Notorious Kingpins

Volume 1

Amado Carrillo Fuentes
Raymond Chow
Khun Sa

By

Ron Chepesiuk

Published in the United States of America by:
Strategic Media Books, Inc.
782 Wofford St.
Rock Hill, SC 29730
www.strategicmediabooks.com

Manufactured in the United States of America.

ISBN-10:1939521643
ISBN-13:9781939521651

Requests for permission should be directed to:
strategicmediabooks@gmail.com

or mailed to:

Permissions
Strategic Media Books, Inc.
782 Wofford St
Rock Hill, SC 29730

Distributed to the trade by:
Cardinal Publishers Group
2402 North Shadeland Ave., Suite A
Indianapolis, IN 46219

TABLE OF CONTENTS

KHUN SA

WARLORD AND HEROIN KINGPIN

PROLOGUE

On the Ropes

In 1967, Khun Sa was riding high. At age 33, the charismatic Burmese warlord had trafficked in opium on his own for a mere three years, but he had been busy consolidating power, grabbing territory, commanding an army of about 2,000 men, and garnering the loyalty and respect of the hill tribes of his native Shan State in Southeast Asia's Golden Triangle region.

Khun Sa's rapid rise, however, put him in conflict with the powerful Kuomintang of China (KMT), the remnants of the military forces defeated by the Chinese Communists under Mao Tse-Tung. The KMT was forced to flee to Burma (present day Myanmar) in 1949. The KMT was also heavily into drug trafficking, and it viewed the upstart Khun Sa as a dangerous rival.

Unfortunately for Khun Sa, he got sucked into a local opium war with the KMT in 1967. Fighting broke out after a Khun Sa caravan of 500 men and 300 mules laden with raw opium set out from the Shan State for Ban Houei Sai in northern Laos. The caravan was to travel across 200 miles of mountain trail and deliver the opium to Laotian General Ouane Rattikone, one of the region's most powerful individuals. The KMT had developed an alliance with the Royal Laotian Army under Rattikone, and he, like Khun Sa, was heavily involved in opium trafficking. The general had also developed a relationship with the CIA during the Vietnam War, which, at this time, was heating up, and he, on the CIA's behest, provided military support against the North Vietnamese Army and the Pathet Lao in Laos' northern region.

What became known as the Opium War heated up when the KMT ambushed Khun Sa's caravan about 50 miles outside Ban Khwan on the Mekong River. Six bombers from the Laotian air force dumped 500-pound bombs on both the Khun Sa forces and the KMT. Then General Rattikone arrived on the scene with his government force, but to the surprise of both Khun Sa and the KMT, the general's forces attacked both sides and took the opium.

The KMT had demanded $250,000 from Rattikone's army to retreat, but it was in no position to negotiate. Under heavy assault, which continued for two days, the KMT fled north for the safety of Laos. Meanwhile, Khun Sa's forces beat a hasty retreat across the Mekong River.

This so-called "Opium War" was an event of global significance. Most importantly, it ultimately boosted the manufacture and export of heroin from the Golden Triangle, making the area of international importance in the illicit drug trade. Also, General Rattikone's victory and his continued involvement in heroin trafficking allowed him to retire a very rich man in 1971.

It looked as if the opium War had delivered a knockout blow to Khun Sa from which he would never recover. But it would not be the last time that his adversaries would count him down for the proverbial ten count. It took time—ten years to be exact—but the Burmese warlord showed remarkable resilience and made a big comeback. Over the coming decades, despite being one of the world's biggest heroin traffickers and the target of local governments, rival ethnic groups, and the CIA, he skillfully projected himself on the world stage as a folk hero, a liberation fighter who stood up for his people, the Shan ethnic minority.

Khun Sa argued that only economic development in the poverty-stricken Shan State could stop opium growing and heroin trafficking. “My people grow opium,” the warlord said. “And they are not doing it for fun. They do it because they need to buy rice to eat and clothes to wear.”

The U.S Drug Enforcement Agency (DEA) and other worldwide anti-narcotics organizations did not buy Khun Sa’s line. Rather, to the good guys, Khun Sa became known as the “Prince of Death” because of the heroin plague he unleashed on the world community. The DEA estimates that, at one point in the 1980s and 1990s, the height of Khun Sa’s power and influence, 60 percent of the heroin being sold on the streets of the U.S. came from opium refined and processed in areas of the Golden Triangle that Khun Sa controlled.

Yet, despite his criminal activities, Khun Sa had the grudging respect of many of his adversaries. In an unguarded moment, for instance, Peter Bourne, an advisor to U.S. President Jimmy Carter, admitted that “Khun Sa was one of the most impressive national figures I have met.”

During his long career as an international drug kingpin, Khun Sa would show time and again that it was better to grudgingly respect him than it was to underestimate him.

☙ ❧

CHAPTER 1

Beginnings

Khun Sa, a pseudonym meaning "Prince Prosperous," began life with few advantages. Indeed, his early years showed no indication that he would become one of history's most infamous drug traffickers. Khun Sa was born in 1934 to a Shan mother and Chinese father in the Shan State village of Hpa Hpeung with the given name of Chang Chi Fu.

The largely rural Shan State, formerly the princedom of Shan, gets its name from the Shan people, one of several ethnic groups that inhabit the area. The state's diverse population is estimated to be between four and six million. The Shan State is the largest state in Burma (present day Myanmar), covering almost a quarter of the total area of Burma. It inhabits parts of Mandalay Region, Kachin State, and Kayin State, as well as adjacent regions of China, Laos and Thailand. The state is situated in the country's northeast where its foothills rise majestically to more than 6,562 feet. Today, vast areas of the state remain largely outside central government control.

In February 1986, Donald Ferrarone, chief of the DEA's Burma office in the 1980s, told "Frontline," the American PBS television program, what he thought of the Shan people and the situation in their state: "I was stationed in Burma in the 1980s and the Shan people had been for years powers in a game that takes place up there that's pretty nasty and that ends up physically and scarring a whole bunch of really nice people. I think they're caught in the middle. The best thing that could happen up there would be for some economic infrastructure to be built and some alternative crops. Things like that."

The Shan people have been engaged in an independence struggle that, for decades, has led to periodic civil war within Burma. Throughout his life, Khun Sa proclaimed himself to be a champion of this movement.

Ferrarone, like many other U.S. officials, did not think too much of Khun Sa's claims that he was fighting for the Shan people. "That's part of the propaganda he's pushed on the innocent people up there," Ferrarone told "Frontline." "They don't believe it. Why should we believe it? Take my word for it."

Khun Sa's father died when he was three years old, and in growing up an orphan, the young boy learned from an early age how to use his wits to survive. The mother did the best she could for her son, even becoming a mistress to a local tax collector from the small town of Mong Tawm in Burma's northern region to make ends meet, but she died as well, two years after marrying. Khun Sa then grew up under the care of his paternal grandfather.

Reportedly the women of the village doted over the boy and treated him as a favorite. In his book, *The Hunt for Khun Sa,* journalist Ron Felber explained, "Their influence (the women of the village) educated him in the ways of women, while his father's resentment taught him the value of discipline, high expectations, and classical cruelty when dealing with enemies."

Khun Sa had three step-brothers who took the Christian names of Oscar, Billy and Morgan. They all went to missionary schools. The details of Khun Sa's personal life are obscure, but it is believed he married a woman named Nan Kyayon, and they had eight children. She died in 1993.

Save for a few years in a Buddhist monastery, Khun Sa did not get much formal education, and he grew up largely illiterate. Noted journalist Bertil Lintner recalled in an article in *Asia Online* that, during one of his interviews with Khun Sa, he noticed that all of the warlord's correspondence had to be read to him and that his replies he sent were dictated.

Still Khun was no country bumpkin. Thomas Dormandy describe Khun Sa's sophistication in his book, *Opium: Reality's Dark Dream*: "He had a cultivated taste in Chinese art, preferring Tang terracottas to nineteenth century kitsch, a good knowledge of history beyond Southeast Asia, and a command of mathematics sufficient to retain a position in global trade."

The chain-smoking warlord, who enjoyed the best French brandy, was a fascinating personality, or as some have said, a fascinating mix of personalities. Khun Sa loved Hollywood, and he especially admired two of its most famous actors: Ronald Reagan and John Wayne. Writer Ron Felber noted that Khun Sa "often imitated John Wayne, donning a diamond-and-sapphire embroidered gun belt, demonstrating a quick-draw like the 'Duke' in the privacy of his bedroom."

Khun Sa loved stories of Jesse James and Billy the Kid and other Wild West outlaws, as well as those of the gangsters from the era of the public enemy, such as Al Capone and John Dillinger, and he watched numerous movies about them.

Khun Sa would make it to Hollywood himself. In the movie "American Gangster," the drug-peddling warlord character is believed to be based on Khun Sa. In the movie, the Khun Sa-based character says, "You think you're going to take 100 kilos of heroin into the U.S.... He must be insane."

Khun Sa loved power and success and admired those who had successfully climbed to the top of the ladder. On one wall of his house, he reportedly hung a photograph of Ross Perot, American billionaire and twice presidential candidate. One of his most prized possessions was a medal bearing the image of King George VI, which was given to Khun Sa's father in recognition of his service to the British Empire.

Not surprisingly, Khun Sa's favorite book was Italian author Niccolò Machiavelli's *The Prince.* According to Felber, one particular Machiavelli maxim was an important guiding principle of his command:

Severities should be dealt with all at once
That by their suddenness they may give less offence
Benefits should be handed out drop by drop
That they may be relished more

While Khun Sa became known for his charm and sense of humor, he could be ruthless and cruel. He killed thousands of people who crossed him and had no qualms causing misery and addiction for millions of people. He even went out of his way to create misery. For instance, he condemned first-time drug offenders under his command to ten days of cold turkey at the bottom an eighteen-foot pit, and chronic offenders to death by a blow to the back of the head.

Felber gives this chilling example of his cruelty: "When bored with his soldier's existence at the jungle compound, he and fifty to sixty of his men would meander out from their supposed hiding place in Chiang Mai, Thailand. Sporting Italian-made and Soviet-made AK47s, they would simply take over the town—nightclubs, discos, entire floors of the 350-room Wiang Inn—commandeering whatever food and liquor they wanted, kidnapping and gang-raping young women at gunpoint, partying for days on end."

When Khun Sa was not causing pain and mayhem, he found time to pursue traditional activities. For instance, at some time in his young adulthood, he became an avid golfer, although it is unclear what his handicap was.

At age 18, Khun Sa began training with the Kuomintang. He then formed his own army or militia, which eventually became known as the Shan United Army, or the Shan State Army. In 1963, thanks largely to the money he made from a number of successful opium shipments to Thailand, he reformed his private army into a Ka Kwe Ye local militia, which at the time numbered about 800 men and was loyal to the Burmese government. In return for Khun Sa's support, the Burmese government gave him money, weapons and uniforms to fight the Shan rebels.

Early in his criminal career, Khun Sa supported Burmese leader General Ne Win (1910-2002), who came to power in 1962 in what was described as a "bloodless" coup. Ne Win was Prime Minister of Burma from 1958 to 1960, and he founded the Burmese Socialist Programme Party in 1962. Win rejected parliamentary democracy as being unsuitable for Burma, and he dissolved the legislature and suspended the country's constitution. Burma has been under military rule ever since.

Ne Win married his criminal activities to local politics, while declaring himself to be a champion of the Shan State people. The strategy worked. Ne Win ruled for 26 years until a coup drove him from power in 1988.

During his lifetime, Khun Sa operated in the Golden Triangle, a 350,000 square kilometer area that includes the mountains of three Asian countries, Laos, Thailand, and Burma, and to a lesser extent the Yunan province in China. The region is coved by forest and inhabited by a tribal clannish population, estimated at 200,000 people, who live in about 300 villages. The Golden Triangle is an area of little government control where the principal means of transportation is the backpack, elephant and mule.

The region's rise to prominence in the international drug trade came soon after World War II. At the time, it was producing less than ten tons of opium a year. But that all changed when the communists, led by Mao Tse-Tung, conquered China in 1949 and clamped down on opium production. The nationalist Chinese (the

Kuomingtang or KMT) fled for the safety of Burma's Shan State in the Golden Triangle, and entered the drug trade in a big way.

Supported by the CIA, the KMT prepared for an invasion of Red China, but the plan never materialized. So it settled into its home and began expanding and monopolizing the opium trade in the Shan State.

According to Alfred McCoy in his book *The Politics of Heroin in Southeast Asia:* "The KMT shipped the opium harvests to northern Thailand where they were sold to General Phao Siyanan, a Thai policeman and CIA client. The CIA had promoted the Phao-KMT partnership to provide a secure area for the KMT, but this alliance soon became a critical factor to the growth of Southeast Asia's narcotics trade."

By the early 1960s, the opium trade was the largest cash crop in the Golden Triangle and an integral part of the northern Thailand economy. The opium production grew from less than 10 tons in the years after World War II to an estimated 300 to 400 tons by 1962. The Bangkok Office of the National Narcotics Control Board estimated that 260 villages in the northern province of Payao, Chiang Mai, Chiang Rai and Mae Hong Son were involved in and economically dependent on the opium trade.

All the countries of the Golden Triangle—Laos and Burma as well as Thailand—got involved in opium cultivation and narcotics trafficking in some form. As one commander of the Nationalist Chinese Fifth Army explained, "We have to fight the evil of communism, and to fight you must have an army, and the army must have guns, and to buy guns, you must have money. In these mountains, the only money is opium."

In 1964, Khun Sa severed his ties with the Burmese army and moved his headquarters from his bases at Lashio and Tang Yang to the east and Ving Ngun in the Wa States, one of Burma's most productive opium-growing areas. Here Khun Sa became strong enough to establish an independent fiefdom that lasted for two years. He increased his wealth and power by setting up a crude refinery that processed raw opium into morphine bricks.

In 1966 he formed another alliance with the Burmese government, a move that allowed him to increase his opium shipments to Thailand and to build his private army to an impressive 2,000-man fighting force. Khun Sa, however, was still not a major drug trafficker. As Alfred McCoy explained, "Khun Sa still controlled only a relatively small percentage of the total opium traffic. A CIA study showed that Khun Sa and other Shan State traffickers were responsible for only seven percent of Burma's heroin production as compared to ninety percent for the KMT."

From a young age, Khun Sa knew how to play the drug smuggling game, and he played it like no other warlord in Southeast Asia. He bribed corrupt senior military commanders in the region to turn a blind eye to his drug smuggling activities. One of them was General Phao, who, by the mid-1950s, headed the largest opium smuggling syndicate in Thailand and was involved in every phase of narcotics trafficking. According to one source, "The level of corruption (created by Phao) was remarkable even by Thai standards."

General Phao had the CIA'S powerful backing, and the agency supplied him with the logistical equipment (aircraft, motor vehicles, and naval vessels) to move the opium from the poppy fields of the Golden Triangle to the sea lanes and beyond.

Phao's CIA-trained Border Patrol Police escorted the opium caravans for the big Thai Chinese drug dealers. Thai Prime Minister Kukrit Pramoj described Phao as "the worse man in all of Thai history, and that's saying a lot!" while the *New York Times* bluntly called the general a "superlative crook."

The CIA's role in the region, especially when it came to opium cultivation and heroin trafficking, cannot be underestimated. The CIA's involvement with drug trafficking in Asia extends back to 1959 and the Chinese Communist Revolution. The CIA supported the Nationalist Communist KMT, which fled China's Yunan Province with arms, ammunition and other supplies.

Historian Alfred McCoy explained that "to retaliate against Communist China for its intervention into the Korean War, President Truman had ordered the CIA to organize these nationalist elements inside Burma for an invasion of China. The idea was that the masses of southwestern China would rise up in revolt against communism, and China would evidently pull its troops out of Korea, and our troops in Korea would be saved. The logic was bizarre, and the records for this operation remain secret, I suspect, because it was one of the most disastrously foolish operations mounted by any agency of the U.S government."

Beginning in the early 1960s, the CIA played an important role in Khun Sa's development as a drug kingpin. Indeed, the CIA support for Khun Sa's drug smuggling operations in the Golden Triangle helped fuel the growing heroin epidemic in the U.S. in the late 1960s and early l970s. While Khun Sa worked as a U.S. drug ally, his heroin was reaching as many as one in seven American soldiers, drug monitoring agencies estimated.

A White House assessment revealed that by 1971 about 34 percent of the U.S. soldiers in South Vietnam were heroin addicts, meaning there were more American heroin addicts in South Vietnam than in the entire U.S. The American soldiers disliked the coarse, brown raw heroin the locals used, and so Khun Sa obligingly turned to manufacturing heroin in the form of a fine powder suitable for intravenous injection.

"This heroin was largely supplied from heroin laboratories operated by U.S. allies, though the White House failed to acknowledge the unpleasant fact," Alfred McCoy pointed out in a 1997 *Progressive* magazine article.

As the Vietnam War wound down, Khun Sa's heroin began to appear on the streets of the U.S. where a kilo of raw opium costing $3,000 in the Golden Triangle could gain as much as $3 million. Meantime, heroin trafficking was corrupting the governments in the region to the point where local police began protecting some of the heroin manufacturing labs.

The U.S. government would eventually put a price on Khun Sa’s head for his drug trafficking ways, but the CIA would quietly continue to support him well after the Vietnam War ended in 1975.

ꝏ ꝏ

CHAPTER 2

War and Prison

By the mid-1960s, Khun Sa was shrewdly mending fences with the Burmese government's support as a strategy to consolidate his power. In one example, Khun Sa persuaded the Burmese government to deputize him as head of a village defense force against the BCP (Burmese Communist Party), the oldest existing party in Burma. The BCP formed alliances with insurgency groups along Burma's (Myanmar's) border with China and was heavily involved in opium cultivation.

The Burmese central government was willing to turn a blind eye to Khun Sa's criminal activities so long as he fought the KMT, the Communist Party of Burma, and its other enemies. For Khun Sa, the alliance allowed him to control a large area in the Shan and Wa States, while he expanded his opium production.

Feeling confident, Khun Sa decided he now had the power to take on his leading rivals, the opium warlords of the KMT. By this time, Khun Sa was on the KMT's radar screen because it was unhappy with his activities in the Shan State. The KMT was particularly disturbed with reports indicating that Khun Sa was buying up huge quantities of opium.

The KMT, moreover, did not appreciate the ultimatum given by the brash warlord. Khun Sa felt he was entitled to the same transit tax that he had to pay the KMT whenever he moved his opium shipments across the border into Laos or Thailand, so he demanded the KMT pay him a similar tax.

In May 1967 the KMT became alarmed when Khun Sa set out from the northern Shan State with a large number of soldiers and a huge sixteen-ton raw opium convoy worth $500,000 wholesale. Along the way, more tribes joined the convoy, and by the time it reached the key city of Kengtung in eastern Shan State, the convoy had 500 men and 300 mules stretching for a mile in a single column.

Khun Sa hoped to use the profits he made from the opium sale to buy about 1,000 new carbines, which would allow him to expand his fighting force to make his army about equal in size to the KMT's Third and Fifth armies. This would put him in a position to threaten the KMT's dominance of the region's drug trade.

The KMT's intelligence network kept a close eye on Khun Sa's caravan movement. By the time it reached Kengtung, the KMT decided it had to intercept the convoy and destroy it. The KMT ambushed Khun Sa's caravan east of Kengtung near the Mekong River, but it escaped and managed to reach Ban Khwan, where the caravan was supposed to deliver the opium to Rattikone's refinery. As the Ban Khwan villagers fled for safety, Khun Sa troops prepared for battle against the KMT.

When the KMT forces reached the village on July 26, 1967, they had a brief skirmish with the Khun Sa forces. The same day, the Laotian provincial commander arrived by helicopter to deliver an ultimatum from General Rattikone to both sides: Get out of Laos now.

The KMT brashly demanded $250,000 for their departure, while Khun Sa radioed a message from Burma, ordering his men to stay put. An intense fire fight broke out the next day. The tide of battle turned when Laotian fighters dropped 500 pound bombs indiscriminately on the KMT and Khun Sa forces.

The KMT fled to Thailand after suffering seventy deaths, but it had to pay General Rattikone an indemnity of $7,500 for the right to return to Thailand. Meanwhile, Khan Sa's men abandoned the opium cargo and fled to Burma, leaving behind eighty-two dead comrades.

While the official story has General Rattikone stealing the load from both Khun Sa's forces and the KMT, sources told journalist Bertil Lintner that Khun Sa had already sold the opium. Whether that was true or not, General Rattikone had clearly won the day.

Meanwhile, Khun Sa's reputation as an important player in the Golden Triangle drug trade was in tatters. "Khun Sa represented the first substantial challenge to KMT control over the Shan states' opium trade—and that challenge was decisively defeated," McCoy assessed. McCoy, however, also notes that the Opium War had a significant long-term impact: "When considered in light of events in the Golden Triangle from 1968 to 1972—particularly the large scale production of number 4 heroin—the 1967 Opium War appears to be a significant turning point in the growth of Southeast Asia's drug traffic."

It now appeared that Khun was finished as a major figure in the region's illicit drug trade. That certainly looked the case when, two years after the Opium War, the Burmese government captured and imprisoned him in Mandalay, Burma's second-largest city. Khun Sa had gone there to negotiate with the Shan rebels, perhaps a prelude to him once again changing sides and opposing the Burmese government.

Khun Sa was charged with treason, arrested and convicted, and he spent the next four years in jail, most of it in solitary confinement. Imprisonment provided the warlord with time for reflection and strategic planning. This was when Khun Sa changed strategy and began to position himself to the Sha nation as a nationalist, a leader who reluctantly trafficked in opium to earn his people's freedom.

Khun Sa, however, was not totally out of the drug trade during this period. His army remained in control of the opium districts to the south of Lashio, the largest town in the northern Shan State, located about 120 miles northeast of Mandalay.

In April 1973, Charlie Win, Khun Sa's second in command, took a force to Taunaggi, the capital of the Shan State, kidnapped two Russian doctors who had come to the Shan capital to inspect a Soviet-built hospital, and demanded Khun Sa's freedom in return for their release. At first, the Burmese government tried to hide the embarrassing incident, but the kidnappers invited a Western film crew to photograph the doctors in their jungle prison. During the next several months, the Burmese government launched several unsuccessful raids looking for the doctors, but could not find them.

Thai General Kriangsak Chamanan was persuaded to step in and negotiate the swap of Khun Sa for the two Russian doctors. Khun Sa was a long-time supporter of the general. Finally, the swap was made, and the doctors were released to the Thai military in June 1974.

After his release, Khun Sa surfaced in northern Thailand in command of an armed force, with headquarters in Ban Hin Taek. In gratitude for arranging his release, Khun Sa gave Winn the ownership and management rights to a front trading company in Chiang Mai where Khun Sa had his weapons and supplies stored.

Khun Sa now focused on re-establishing his powerful position in the Golden Triangle drug trade. The warlord was primed for a remarkable comeback.

ಌ ಌ

PHOTOS

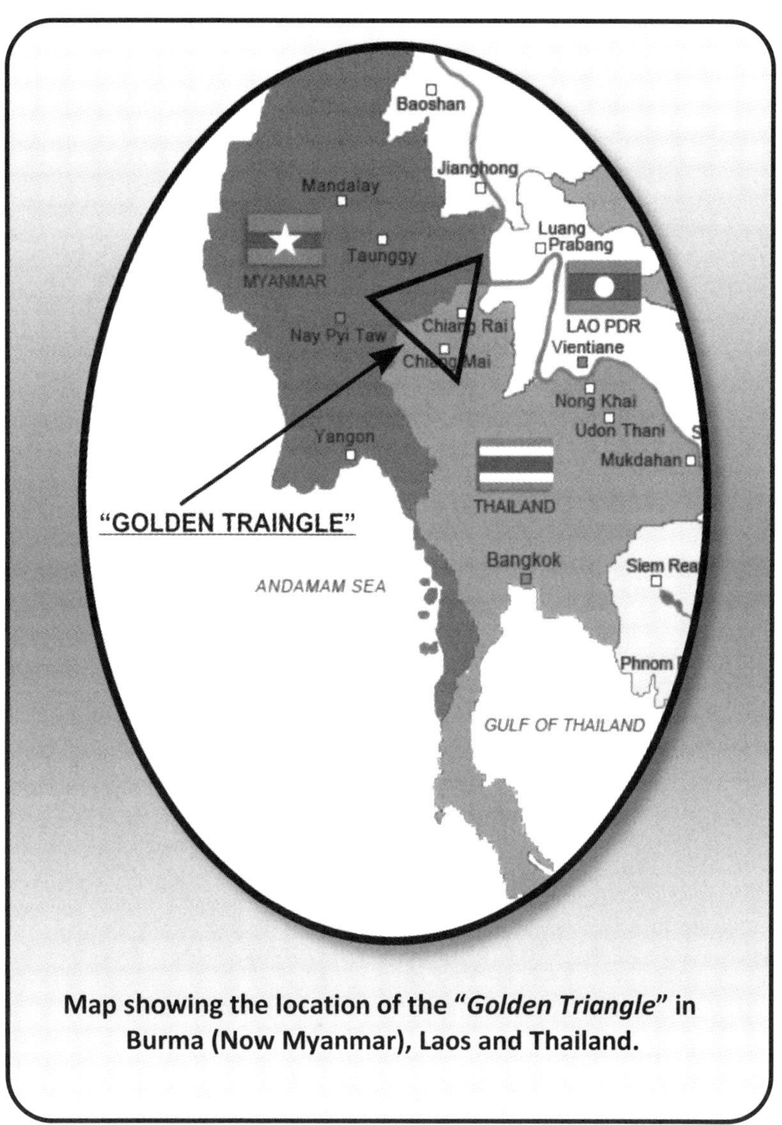

Map showing the location of the "*Golden Triangle*" in Burma (Now Myanmar), Laos and Thailand.

Khun Sa during his apogee years

Khun Sa's army

Khun Sa's opium after a bust-and-destroy operation

Khun Sa's Army during the "Opium War" fighting the Kuomintang of China (KMT)

Khun SA in later years surrounded by his body guards

Burma, Laos and Thailand's "*Golden Triangle*" poppy plants from which heroin is extracted

View of Khun Sa's camp in Hian-Taek now a museum

Khun Sa's quarters in the camp

Monument to Khun Sa in the camp at Hian-Taek

Khun Sa during house arrest and prior to his death due to a Heroin overdose when he was 73 years old

Khun Sa - Chan Shee Fu with Bangkok blogger, Andrew Drummond, Homong, Burma, 1988

ဆ ဃ

CHAPTER 3

Comeback

General Kriangsak Chamanan took office as Thailand's Prime Minister in 1977, and judging by his public statements, Khun Sa had nothing to worry about when it came to his drug trafficking activities. Prime Minister Kriangsak criticized his predecessor's anti-narcotics campaign and said it was up to the U.S., not Thailand, to solve the narcotics problem.

In an obvious jab at Uncle Sam, Kriangsak told the *Bangkok Post* on April 10, 1977, "Those who criticize Thailand for corruption should also look into the corruption in other official circles, which has made it possible for the narcotics trade to flourish in many countries." Kriangsak was telling Uncle Sam to take a good hard look in the mirror.

Critics, especially those in the U.S. jumped on Kriangsak, charging that the Prime Minister was corrupt and that he had ties to the region's drug trade. In retrospect, at least one major news media source disagreed. *The Economist* magazine, in fact, stated that the general deserved a note of credit.

According to *The Economist,* Kriangsak “seems to have remained an honest man in an army famous for its corruption, running smuggling rackets across the country's borders, and lining the pockets of generals who became involved in business.”

But Kriangsak changed his tune about Khun Sa. He simply could not tolerate the warlord’s desire to be a public figure or his bragging in the press, which drew embarrassing attention to the Golden Triangle’s drug trade. In one interview with a Bangkok newspaper, Khun Sa dubbed himself “King of the Golden Triangle.” While acknowledging the damage the illicit drug trade has done, Khun Sa said he did not feel in the least guilty. In fact, he claimed that the drug trade was justified, given the serious problems facing his people.

"In the past 17 years, the Western world has lost a lot of money on drug suppression, spent thousands of millions of dollars for nothing," Khun Sa said. "Instead, they should help people out of their misery."

Khun Sa went further, proclaiming that he, himself, could stop cold the illicit traffic in drugs. Political leaders abroad took him seriously and began treating him like a statesman, not just a drug trafficker. Westerners even traveled to the wilds of the Golden Triangle to meet the warlord at his base in Ban Hin Taek, located just inside Thailand.

In 1977, Khun Sa approached U. S. Congressman Lester Wolff with a proposed deal: money in return for his withdrawal from the international drug trade. The U.S. government quickly rejected the offer because, as one U.S. official put it, "The United States didn't then, and still does not, engage in talks with a 'rebel' who is engaged in fighting a government that Washington recognizes as legitimate."

In January 1988, Khun Sa again tried to strike a deal by using an emissary, Phra Chamroon Parnchand, an abbot active in the fight against drug addiction in Thailand. Through Phra Chamroon, Khun Sa proposed to put an end to the Golden Triangle drug trade in return for U.S. economic assistance of U.S. $95 million a year for six years. The U.S. again rejected the offer.

U.S. official Peter Bourne claimed that he "found not a single person who felt this concept had any validity." Bourne explained: "It is unthinkable that any representative of this administration would negotiate with representatives of insurgent groups opposed to the legitimate government of Burma, much less use the American taxpayers' dollars for a program that would, in effect, provide a subsidy for narcotic traffickers and arms for an insurrection. The so-called Shan United Army is led by a ruthless band of ethnic Chinese opium warlords."

By 1980 Khun Sa's presence in Thailand had become an embarrassment to the Thai government, and he was ordered to leave the country. Khun Sa complied, moving his base of operation eleven miles down the road to a location inside Burma, only to return a few months later to Ban Hin Taek, a village in the Chai Rai area in northern Thailand.

Angered by Khun Sa's recalcitrance, the Thai government put a price on his head, while its military bombed his base. Then, in October 1981, Thai forces, with the help of Burmese guerrillas, tried to assassinate Khun Sa. But the warlord was given ample warning, and the hit failed. Finally, the following year, Thai military forces undertook a full scale assault and overran Ban Hin Taek.

The aggressive campaign to take down Khun Sa made life difficult for him, but it was just for a short period of time, and he was able to regroup. Khun told one interviewer how he did it: "I continued to strengthen my position and build several scattered fortresses and bastions. Steadily the size of the rank and file increased, until it was 6,000 strong. These soldiers under the leadership of my trusted aides were divided into numerous smaller units and scattered throughout the Shan State near the Thai border. Refineries were set up, and I began the shipment of various grades of heroin."

Despite being a hunted man, Khun Sa had no intention of staying out of the limelight. During the 1980s, he continued to meet with journalists who were willing to trek through the jungle to see him. Khun Sa eventually was based at Homong, Burma, where he lived in a wooden house that was surrounded with heavily armed soldiers and 50-caliber anti-aircraft machine guns.

In September 1990, Charles Wallace, a *Los Angeles Times* journalist, gave a revealing report of what he learned about Khun Sa's life at Homong: "He is said to have a compound with three homes, to which he does not invite foreign guests. He has spent money acquiring a collection of beautiful horses. He has a wife and five grown children, among them a daughter who reportedly was educated in England under a pseudonym. These days, Khun Sa travels around in a white Toyota pickup truck accompanied by 10 bodyguards toting U.S.-made automatic weapons, including a roof-mounted, 50-caliber heavy machine gun. He wears no jewelry other than a stainless steel Rolex watch and carries a rough-hewn, thick wooden cane."

In 1988, Khun Sa met with Australian journalist Stephen Rice, who had crossed the border from Thailand into Burma illegally. The warlord told Rice he was willing to sell his entire crop to the Australian government for about $40 million annually for the next eight years. Drug trafficking experts said the offer, if accepted, would have enabled the U.S. and Australian governments to stop drugs coming into their counties. But once again a Western country rejected Khun Sa's offer.

The following year, after his indictment by a New York court for trying to smuggle 1000 tons of heroin into the U.S., Khun Sa had an interview with Canadian journalist Patricia Elliott, who was on assignment for *The Bangkok Post*. Khun Sa told the journalist he would eradicate the opium crop for U.S. $200 million in U.N. assistance, U.S. $265 million in foreign investment, and US $89.5 million in private aide. In return, he wanted a program of education, health care and crop reduction for his people.

According to official U.S. estimates, the Golden Triangle's opium crop in the 1988-89 growing season amounted to 2,600 tons, about 85 percent of it from Burma. Meanwhile, Khun Sa controlled 70 percent of the heroin trade in the Golden Triangle and an estimated 40 to 45 percent of the heroin smuggled into the U.S. The U.S. reportedly considered the offer but rejected it

Not all journalists who met with Khun Sa were as lucky as Stephen Rice. At least one, in fact, did not live to tell about it. A Thai journalist went looking for Khun Sa to interview him about the murder of two suspected informants and the wife of a DEA agent in broad daylight on the main street in Chiang Rai. The journalist was found murdered.

Khun Sa's most controversial visitor was James Bo Gritz, a former U.S. Army Special Forces officer and Vietnam War veteran and a former Grand Wizard of the Ku Klux Klan. Gritz was interested in trying to find the whereabouts of U.S. prisoners of war (POWs). In 1986 he went to see Khun Sa to find out what he knew. Gritz returned to the U.S. with a bombshell videotaped interview in which Khun Sa implicated several officials of the Reagan administration in narcotics trafficking in Southeast Asia. Gritz believed these officials were also involved in the cover up of the status and whereabouts of American POWs.

One of the prominent U.S. officials that Gritz identified was Richard Armitage, the Deputy Secretary of State during George W. Bush's first presidential term. Armitage was also Assistant Secretary of Defense for International Security Policy during the first term of Ronald Reagan's administration. One of Armitage's responsibilities was the recovery of MIAs and POWs from Vietnam. After meeting with Khun Sa, Gritz came to believe that Armitage used his position to block private efforts like that of Gritz's to find and bring home missing American servicemen.

In testifying before Congress on June 30, 1987, Gritz said: "I and three other Americans have met with Khun Sa. We all believe him to be sincere, certainly in view of the dismal failure of the CIA and DEA to slow, stop and even deter the flow of drugs from the

Golden Triangle. It seems a change is in order, especially since Khun Sa has directly implicated persons within the CIA as some of his best customers.

Khun Sa told Gritz in the videotape interview that Armitage and other Americans were involved in drug trafficking between 1965 to at least 1979, and they used the profits to fund anti-communist operations. Armitage denied the allegations, describing them as “ludicrous and baseless.” It should be noted that he was never charged with any crimes.

Instead of negotiating a settlement with Khun Sa, the U.S. turned the warlord into one of the world’s most wanted criminals. In 1989 Uncle Sam indicted him on drug charges and put a $2 million reward on his head for information leading to his arrest and conviction in a U.S. court.

Shortly after being indicted, the New York City Attorney, who filled the indictment, received a bomb in the mail. Police defused the bomb, and Khan Sa became the prime suspect. But within 24 hours of the bomb’s discovery, Khun Sa called the district attorney from Thailand to deny he had anything to do with the bomb.

In the 1980s, the U.S. government focused on giving the Burmese government financial and material aid to spray the opium fields. The move, however, ostensibly backfired. Farmers were scared into greatly increasing their planting instead of reducing production. The spraying also ruined thousands of acres of useful farmland and poisoned the countryside with herbicides.

Meanwhile, during the 1980s, Khun Sa consolidated his power. In 1985, he formed an alliance with the Tai Revolutionary Council of Mohr Hang, which allowed him to gain control of a large area along the Thai-Burma border. The Moong Tai Army was founded in 1985 after the merging of two rebel factions; the Shan United Army (SUA) and the Mohr Hang-faction of the Shan United Revolutionary Army (SURA). By the 1990s, the Moong Tai Army at its peak had strength of 20,000 soldiers.

Khun Sa now had more than an army. There was also a separate political movement, known as the Tai Revolutionary Council, as well as a governing executive committee, schools, hospitals and a force of political workers and tax collectors.

Through the 1980s and into the 1990s, Khun Sa continued to battle Thai troops along the Thailand-Burma border, as well as Burmese troops in the Shan states. Yet Khun Sa managed to hold his own. "We were fighting him for years," one Burmese colonel told the *New York Times*. "We're not gaining much ground because he was well-equipped, well dug in and the terrain was terrible. We were sacrificing too many casualties."

While battling his many enemies, Khun Sa acted more like a head of state than a wanted criminal. The warlord was so confident of his position that in December 1993 he invited Thai military intelligence officers to his New Year's Eve bash, even though the government of Thailand had put a price on his head.

The reality was—no one was seriously looking for Khun Sa because he was able to use his drug money to pay off Burmese and Thai army officials and politicians. Meanwhile, the U.S. government, despite its public declarations, was more interested in containing the Burmese communists than it was in taking down a drug lord.

But the Burmese government did occasionally try. For instance, as Khun Sa prepared for his New Year's Eve bash in December 1993, the Burmese government dispatched 8,000 troops to wage war on him. In a fierce exchange of mortar shells and machine-gun fire for more than four hours, Khun Sa lost twenty men and the Burmese troops about one hundred. Thousands of people in villages near the Thai border had to flee.

The DEA also tried to take down Khun Sa. Occasionally, the agency claimed success. In early 1992, for example, the DEA nabbed Lin Chien Pang, one of Khun Sa's chief lieutenants, in Malaysia and persuaded Malaysian authorities to hold him pending extradition to New York. But a Malaysian judge ruled against extradition and Pang was freed. The U.S. government appealed the case, but lost.

By the mid-1990s, Khun Sa had come a long way in the cut throat world of drug trafficking. Indeed, it seemed like nothing his enemies did could diminish his power and influence. For the U.S. government he had become the most dangerous and formidable adversary in its emerging War on Drugs.

ဆ ဆ

CHAPTER 4

Operation Tiger Trap

By the early 1990s Khun Sa was a powerful opium kingpin who oversaw a criminal empire based in the poppy fields blanketing the mountains of eastern Burma. The warlord commanded a private militia of 20,000 soldiers, and given the politics and economics of Southeast Asia, he was considered untouchable.

Still, Khun Sa's climb to power has not been an easy one. He had to survive an opium war, assassination attempts, a U.S. indictment, the enmity of the governments bordering the Golden Triangle, and international notoriety that made him one of the world's most wanted criminals.

With the constant threat of death, Khun Sa remained philosophical about his fate, even chuckling as he told one reporter, "If Khun Sa is captured and killed and the opium problem is settled, then Khun Sa deserves to die. But with Khun Sa's death, do you think this opium problem will be settled? I somehow doubt it."

Despite several unsuccessful attempts to negotiate a settlement with Uncle Sam that had begun in 1977, Khun Sa still kept trying. In 1993, for instance, the warlord sent another letter to Uncle Sam, this time to the newly elected president, Bill Clinton. It was a familiar message. He could stop opium cultivation if the U.S. and the international community would help his people switch to an alternative livelihood.

"People grow poppies because they are neglected by the Burmese government," Khun Sa's letter stated. He believed that if the Burmese withdrew from the Shan State, "the Shan would voluntarily pull up the opium poppies by their roots."

The Clinton administration dismissed the proposal as a publicity stunt. As one narcotics officer explained to the *Times of London* newspaper, "He (Khun Sa) is no Robin Hood. He is one hell of a bad guy. There is no way we are going to have a deal with him."

Khun Sa looked invincible, but in 1994 his fortunes began to change dramatically, largely because of three major developments. First, the DEA's high profile kingpin strategy in which it went after the top dog in a criminal drug organization appeared to be working. In 1989, the U.S. government identified General Manuel Noriega, the President of Panama, as a drug trafficker, and he was indicted.

In December of that year, the U.S. invaded Panama and arrested or kidnapped Noriega—depending upon your point of view—and took him back to the U.S. for trial. In 1992 Noriega was convicted and sent to prison for forty years (later reduced to thirty).

Then the following year, Colombian security forces, with the help of the U.S., cornered Pablo Escobar in an apartment complex in Medellin, Colombia, and gunned down the so-called "World's Greatest Outlaw." The take down effectively ended the Medellin Cartel's prominence in the international drug trade.

Secondly, under pressure from Uncle Sam, Thailand and Burma, countries in which Khun Sa operated, changed their policies toward the warlord. Khun Sa had operated in an open environment, but the Thai government closed down its side of the border with the Golden Triangle to Khun Sa, depriving his forces of vital goods and services. Meanwhile, the Burmese government, under pressure from the U.S., began to step up its military operations against Khun Sa.

The third and most important factor was the U.S.'s decision to go after Khun Sa in a major initiative known as Operation Tiger Trap. In an interview with "Frontline," the television program, in February 1996, Don Ferranone, Chief of the DEA's Bangkok office from 1993 to 1996, revealed that the DEA had concluded it needed to do more if it was to stop the heroin trafficking from Southeast Asia. And in doing more, the DEA needed some help.

"We needed to open up a lot of avenues, and we needed to get a lot more help," Ferranone explained. "And that included help to shut down the resupply of the Shan United Army that was going on at the border between Thailand and Burma. There was a flood of essential war material, ammunition, weapons, cement, steel, trucks, medicine...you name it, that was coming across the border day and night, unimpeded, and driven by cash from sales of heroin into the European and American market. So we had to somehow close that down."

To do that, the DEA devised a plan with the help of first the Thais and eventually the Burmese government. Devised in the DEA's Bangkok office in June 1994, Operation Tiger was an international multi-agency anti-drug operation designed to take down what was considered the world's largest heroin trafficking organization: Khun Sa's Shan United Army (SUA). The DEA considered Operation Tiger Trap to be its most ambitious project to date in its effort to disrupt heroin trafficking in Southeast Asia.

Tiger Trap was divided into phases, and it relied on every available tool in both the American and Thai anti-criminal arsenals. The operation linked up the District Attorney's Office in the Eastern District of New York and the DEA office in New York City. As Ferranone explained, "Every person in Khun Sa's distribution network would be raided in an attempt to pick up documentary evidence and basically to run a bowling ball down the middle of his (Khun Sa's) operation."

Burma joined the alliance because the country's military junta believed Khun Sa had become too powerful, and it was worried about the warlord's desire to have an independent Shan State. The Thai government played a vital role in the operation by closing the border and cutting off the flow of the precursor chemicals used in heroin manufacturing, and the vital supplies, such weapons, cement, steel, gasoline, trucks and food that Khun Sa's forces needed to function. The coordinated and lightning-quick implemented plan also cut off Khun Sa's money and customers and threatened to throw the Khun Sa organization into chaos.

As Operation Tiger Trap took shape, Khun Sa began to have problems within his own ranks. After a skirmish with the Burmese army in April 1995, many in the Khun Sa army began to desert, complaining that the warlord was more interested in drug trafficking than he was in the cause of Shan independence.

By October, 1994, Khun Sa was on the ropes. Under pressure from the U.S., Thailand sealed its border, and thousands of his followers tried to flee his stronghold at Homong, Burma. Khun Sa depended on Thailand for supplies, and he was forced to have his people track through the jungle on ten-hour-long trips to smuggle goods back to Homong from the black market on the border. In a two-month period, the price of rice more than tripled. "The man (Khun Sa) is finished," one unidentified source familiar with the Operation Tiger Trap told *Reuters*.

The pressure worked, and Thai authorities began making busts. In early November 1994, for instance, after a brief shootout on a highway in Chiang Mai province, about 390 miles from Bangkok, Thai police arrested two Thai citizens and seized weapons believed destined for Khun Sa. Police said the weapons were smuggled across the Thai border from Cambodia.

It was an important bust. If the insurgents had gotten hold of the weapons, it would mean they would have had the enhanced capability to shoot down American aircraft.

Then on November 27, 1994, teams comprised of the Royal Thai Police, Thai Special Forces, narcotics agents and U.S. DEA agents lured targets in Burma to cross the border into Thailand where they were arrested. When law enforcement authorities had completed their operations, thirteen senior SUA officials were in jail and facing indictments in the Eastern District of New York.

"These guys were his brothers, his brain trust," one official told *Newsweek* magazine. "They handled the money, made the deals to keep the business going."

But the arrest of the so-called "Dirty 13" suspects created controversy in Thailand. Critic charged that their arrests constituted a significant infringement of Thai sovereignty because they involved the arrest of Thai nationals.

The evidence collected and the witnesses indicted were used to re-indict Khun Sa and his entire criminal infrastructure. As Ferranone explained, "For the first time we had witnesses in our hands who were able actually to document and testify to the involvement of Khun Sa, his chief of refinery operations, his various station chiefs...his brothers and his transportation people...all the way to New York City."

The authorities would eventually go after Khun Sa's family. In 1996, Apitummakoob Apawee, Khun Sa's daughter, was arrested and charged with helping her father hide millions of dollars in drug proceeds. Apawee was reported to be one of Khun Sa's thirty children. But the charges were dropped in early September 1996 after the prosecution unsuccessfully sought more time to investigate the $33 million found deposited in Japanese bank accounts in the daughter's name. Apawee claimed the money was donated to Khun Sa's Shan Liberation Army by a Taiwanese businessman, who was described as a close friend of the warlord's.

The authorities returned to the daughter jade worth $1 million, gold jewelry, a Rolex watch and an apartment. Apowee returned to Thailand to live with her mother.

"We can prove the funds went to a drug trafficker, but we can't prove they were proceeds from drug trafficking," said U.S. prosecutor Lynne Shine.

It was not only Khun Sa who was feeling the heat. In early October 1994, the Shan National People's Liberation Party, a Shan insurgent organization of nearly 1800 men, laid down their arms and surrendered to the Burmese government at Sesat, about seventy miles southeast of Taunggyi, the Shan State capital. According to Burmese military officials, the surrender left the Shan State free of insurgents for the first item in forty-six years. Only Khun Sa, a drug dealer, remained a threat to peace in the region.

Even though Operation Tiger Trap was tightening the noose around Khun Sa's neck, the warlord remained defiant, even cocky. He declared himself to be President of the Shan State Restoration Council and still maintained that the people from his homeland would only stop growing opium when they gained their freedom.

But Khun Sa was feeling the heat, and he was running out of options. In 1994 he offered to surrender after a report in the *New York Times* revealed that Burma's military leaders offered Uncle Sam a deal: They would arrest Khun Sa if the U.S. lifted its arms embargo of Burma. The Clinton administration considered the proposal, but rejected it, largely because of its dislike for Burma's dictatorial junta and its human rights record.

It became apparent that Khun Sa was willing to surrender, but only on his terms. Otherwise, it looked like he would not go down without a fight. Still the anti Khun Sa coalition kept up the pressure. In mid-October 1994, heavy fighting between the Burmese government and guerrillas loyal to Khun Sa broke out in eastern Burma and continued for more than two weeks. Khun Sa now faced the serious threat of thousands of Burmese troops attacking his base at Homong, Burma. One guerrilla source told *Reuters* that sixty-seven Burmese troops had been killed in the fighting while Khun Sa's casualties were small.

Word circulated that this threat would force Khun Sa to relocate his headquarters from the southern Shan State near the border with Thailand to the eastern Shan State near the Mekong River, which forms the border between Burma and Laos

Khun Sa was now cornered, and he had no escape routes. He was boxed in with hostile China to the north, Thailand to the south, rival drug lords and enemies to the east and a battalion of Burmese soldiers advancing on his stronghold in eastern Burma. Moreover, he would eventually have to face the full force of the Burmese military because the Burmese government had reached peace agreements with the country's rebel groups.

In November 1995, Khun Sa sent a message to the Burmese military, announcing his intention to retire as commander of his army and become a chicken farmer. Khun Sa's surrender finally came in May 1996 in a surreal ceremony. Khun Sa welcomed the leader of the Burmese army and government officials to his home, where the two parties exchanged Scotch whiskey and gifts as they posed for photographs.

Everybody was polite. Before a television camera, Khun Sa told General Kyaw Ba, "If I have done anything, please forgive me." The general replied, "We must forgive him (Khun Sa) because he surrendered and he has given us no problems."

Eventually, 12,000 of Khun Sa's troops surrendered with their weapons. It looked like Khun Sa was finished as a warlord. The press speculated that, with Khun Sa's total defeat, he would surely be sentenced to a long prison term. Yet, remarkably, Khun Sa still had cards to play.

☙ ❧

CHAPTER 5

The End

After surrendering, Khun Sa retired to Rangoon, Burma, and virtually disappeared from public view. He was protected by Burma's secret intelligence service and ostensibly under house arrest, which meant his access to the media was limited. Yet, reports leaked out about how the old warlord was doing. His health was poor, and he suffered from a variety of ailments that included diabetes, partial paralysis and high blood pressure, but it was reported that was living in luxury with four young Shan mistresses and that he was living a quiet life in which he loved to raise angora rabbits and play with his grandchildren.

Khun Sa had laundered his money well and had made substantial investments in real estate, a ruby mine, and even in a toll road linking Rangoon to Mandalay. So money was no problem for him.

Many observers believed that the former warlord was still in the drug trafficking business, given the corruption that existed in Southeast Asia. One member of the Khun Sa army told *Reuters* that his former leader "had paid millions to a general to guarantee his peaceful retirement after his surrender."

Many U.S. officials did not say it publically, but they believed that Khun Sa had worked out a deal with his Burmese captors that allowed him to stay active in the drug trade.

So what was the public to make of what was supposed to be Khun Sa's "retirement?" Writing in *Asia Online* on November 1, 2007, Bert Lintner concluded, "In reality, Khun Sa was never 'captured', he gave himself up in exchange for a lucrative deal for himself and his family. And there never was a dent made in the narcotics trade he promoted. If Khun Sa's network proved anything, it was that the networks that controlled the trade were able to survive even without their so called kingpins."

U.S. officials were disappointed in how the Burmese government treated Khun Sa, in reality more like a distinguished citizen than a drug kingpin. They did have a point. Consider that Burmese government officials stopped characterizing Khun Sa as a "terrorist" and began referring to him as "Mr. Khun Sa."

Khun Sa's former colleagues said he had surrendered in part to escape the 1989 criminal charges in the U.S. where he was indicted for trying to import 1,000 tons of heroin to the U.S. The U.S. wanted him to stand trial in the U.S., but all of Uncle Sam's extradition requests were refused. So the U.S. government announced a $2 million reward for information leading to his arrest and conviction in the U.S.

In June 2000, the U.S. government made public the names of the twelve international drug kingpins. On the list was Khun Sa, even though he had surrendered four years earlier. The list was really an effort by Uncle Sam to make a public statement. Do business with these criminal drug kingpins and/or their associates and risk the possibility of going to jail. Violating the law could mean a fine of $1 million in administrative penalties, court-imposed penalties of as much as ten years in prison, and up to $10 million in fines for individuals.

The U.S. never did bring Khun Sa to justice. On October 26, 2000, he died in Rangoon at age 73. The cause of death was not stated. Khun Sa was secretly cremated. Remarkably, while officially captured and detained, Khun Sa was never charged with a crime.

Within a couple of weeks of Khun Sa's death, a memorial service was planned. Interestingly, the memorial's primary aim was to boost tourism in the region. Various Thai state agencies were willing to work together to help make the memorial possible.

While Khun Sa reposed in forced retirement, the international drug trade changed. It is true the Golden Triangle remained a source of the heroin sold on the streets of the United States, but new drug lords have appeared on the scene to fill the void left by his takedown. Most importantly, Afghanistan replaced Burma as the key source for most of the world's opium. The UN estimated that Afghanistan was now responsible for 92 percent of the world's opium. With the help of Chinese investment, Burma is replacing opium with other crops, such as tea and rubber.

Khun Sa's legacy is now part of history. Today, visitors to the Chiang Mai Province of Thailand can visit the Khun Sa Museum in Ban Toed Thai, situated on Khun Sa's original camp headquarters. The Museum's web site states that "the buildings have been tidied up after a flood caused significant damage and loss of relics from the original occupancy."

There is still plenty to see in the museum. Among the relics on view are Khun Sa's military uniform, his walking stick and sword, and sculpture of Khun Sa that shows him seated with legs crossed at the table where he received distinguished guests. Overnight and multi-day trips are available, which allow tourists to explore northern Thailand, the area around the museum.

Today, the world has not forgotten Khun Sa and his criminal legacy. He remains infamous for being one of the most powerful—if not the most powerful—drug kingpin of all time. In February 1996, DEA agent Don Ferranone told *Frontline*, "When you look at the universe of major trafficking organizations throughout the world, he fits in there with the top five."

If Khun Sa were still alive today, he would most likely be proud of that status.

ꕥ ꕥ ꕥ ꕥ

LORD OF THE SKIES

The Story of
AMADO CARRILLO FUENTES
Drug Kingpin

PROLOGUE

DEADLY HIT

By all accounts, the man known as the Lord of the Skies should have been dead. Amado Carrillo Fuentes, the biggest drug dealer in México, maybe the world, along with his wife and six children, were dining at the Ochoa Bali Hai Restaurant, a chic seafood eatery in México City, when nearly a dozen stone-cold killers marched through the front door looking for him. They carried cases, which they opened to unload their machine guns and blast away.

It happened so quickly that Carrillo Fuentes' bodyguards could not react. As Carrillo Fuentes, his family, and shocked diners dove for cover, three of the drug lord's eight bodyguards were cut down in the hail of bullets.

An architect was also dining at the restaurant, and mistaking him for Carrillo Fuentes, their target, the killers riddled him with bullets. The Carrillo Fuentes family cowered under a table amidst the carnage. Finally, the shooting stopped. Satisfied that they had gotten their target, the hit squad turned around, marched out of the restaurant and drove off.

Later when the police arrived, none of the people in the restaurant could say for certain what exactly happened. And Carrillo Fuentes was not available to talk because, in the ensuing confusion, he, his family, and the surviving bodyguards casually walked out of the restaurant.

Five people were killed in the shootout and two others wounded. An innocent bystander waiting outside the restaurant for the valet to deliver his automobile was gunned down and killed. Martin Martínez Pantaleon, a 30-year old police officer, was also murdered trying to stop Carrillo Fuentes and his entourage from fleeing. The drug lord's driver ran over Martínez with their car, and then sprayed him with machine gun fire.

In a twist of fate, the low profile kept by Carrillo Fuentes saved his life. The Mexican authorities and Carrillo Fuentes' enemies knew who he was—the country's most notorious drug kingpin, a ruthless gangster whom *Forbes* magazine had recognized as one of the world's richest men, with a fortune estimated at nearly $25 billion. Carrillo Fuentes' nickname was Lord of the Skies, recognition of his pioneering use of old passenger jets to move multi-ton loads of cocaine from Colombia to México.

But only four photos of the drug lord were known to exist, and the fact that Carrillo Fuentes changed his appearance like some prima donnas change their apparel made the photos essentially worthless as a means of identification.

Moreover, Amado Carrillo Fuentes had corrupted a significant part of the establishment, from the country's presidency to the Mexican man and woman cop in the street, and this sad state of affairs made the drug lord virtually untouchable. Mexican drug traffickers also knew the Lord of the Skies because they had joined him in what became known as the Mexican Federation, a loosely knit smuggling cooperative in which Carrillo Fuentes and the members shared equipment, intelligence and smuggling routes instead of trying to kill each other. Colombia's drug kingpins from the country's powerful Medellín and Cali cartels knew Carrillo

Fuentes because they had forged strategic alliances with him to move their illicit product to the drug-demand market in the U.S.

The U.S. authorities knew him, too, for his use of jumbo Boeing 727 airplanes to move tons of cocaine to the U.S. market and millions of dollars out of the U.S. to safe money laundering banking havens worldwide.

Soon after the attempted hit, speculation abounded as to who was behind it. One theory fingered Colombia's powerful Cali Cartel. It was true that the cartel had a close working relationship with Carrillo Fuentes, but their relationship suddenly soured in August 1993 when the Mexican navy seized more than nine tons of cocaine off the coast of Mazatlán, a Mexican resort town in the Sinaloa state. The Cali Cartel lost $20 million on the botched drug run, and it blamed an informant in Carrillo Fuentes' organization. But then the speculation went, Carrillo Fuentes was too valuable a partner, so the Cali Cartel swallowed its loss and quickly patched things up.

The authorities soon had a better suspect. Word leaked that the hitmen were actually badge-carrying cops on the payroll of Juan García Abrego, the powerful leader in México's Gulf Cartel and a bitter rival of Carrillo Fuentes. At the time, Garcia Abrego was México's most wanted drug lord and on the FBI's 10 Most Wanted List, with a U.S. reward offer of $2 million for his capture. Yet, despite being hunted, García Abrego wanted Carrillo Fuentes out of the way, snitches told authorities, and so he had arranged the hit.

But although Carrillo Fuentes had a reputation for being a gangster who favored negotiating over assassination, the authorities knew Carrillo Fuentes' penchant for violence. The assassins had broken an unwritten rule of the Mexican drug smuggling world: Never mess with a rival's family. Carrillo Fuentes' wife had been injured in the attack, and, no doubt, Amado Carrillo Fuentes would seek revenge.

☙ ❧

CHAPTER 1

BEGINNINGS

Amado Carrillo Fuentes was born to the drug smuggling life to Vicente Carrillo and Aurora Fuentes on December 17, 1953, in Guamuchulito, Navolato, Sinaloa State, México, an area that has produced many drug smugglers. Published accounts report that Amado was one of fourteen children, while American intelligence put the number of his family offspring at eight or nine. None of those details, however, can be verified. Carrillo Fuentes' anonymity and the confusion about his background would envelope the Lord of the Skies like a protective cover throughout his criminal career and pose a challenge for law enforcement.

Later, one U.S. law enforcement official would say this about Carrillo Fuentes: "To tell you the truth, we're just not getting much intelligence about him because no one is talking. His circle is small and everybody else is afraid to tell us anything."

It is certain that Amado's nephews and nieces were the offspring of Ernesto Fonseca Carrillo, aka Don Nieto, a Guadalajara Cartel leader. Formed in the 1980s by Uncle Ernesto, Rafael Caro

Quintero and Miguel Angel Félix Gallardo, the powerful Guadalajara Cartel shipped tons of heroin and Raphael Caro Quintero to the United States. The cartel prospered from its relationship with the Medellín and Cali cartels, being among the first of the Mexican drug trafficking groups to work with the Colombians.

Uncle Ernesto took young Amado under his wing and sent him to tend marijuana fields in Zacatecas. In his uncle, the kid had a powerful mentor. Fonseca Carrillo had assumed leadership of the so-called Juárez Cartel in 1985 after its leader Rafael Aguilar Guajardo was gunned down in Cancun.

Uncle Ernesto achieved notoriety in 1985 when he was fingered for the murder of Enrique Camarena, a Mexican-born American DEA undercover agent who was abducted on February 7, 1985, while on assignment in México, and then tortured and murdered.

In response to this outrageous act, the DEA launched *Operation Leyenda*, the largest homicide investigation in its history. Pressured by the U.S., Mexican authorities quickly apprehended Fonseca Carrillo.

After his apprenticeship working in the marijuana fields, young Amado began moving up the criminal ladder. He worked at loading marijuana onto trucks and driving the product to safe houses before becoming a small-time marijuana smuggler using mule carts and melon trucks. By the 1980s, he was using twin-engine planes to move marijuana and cocaine to market.

Most likely, Amado's uncle introduced Amado to members of México's number one drug smuggling family at the time: The Herreras. Headed by Jaime Herrera Nevarez, a functionally illiterate ex-cop, the Herrera family became notorious as the biggest Mexican heroin distributor to the Chicago drug market. Carrillo Fuentes reportedly helped tend the Herreras' opium fields, all the while learning as much as he could about the illicit drug trade.

Carrillo Fuentes then made his way to the Chihuahua State where he received an important apprenticeship from one of

México's most charismatic drug traffickers, Pablo Acosta Villarreal, nicknamed *El Zorro de Ojinaga* ("the Ojinaga Fox") At the height of his power, Acosta Villarreal controlled a 200-mile stretch of the U.S.-Mexican border. At first Acosta Villarreal only distributed marijuana and heroin, but near the end of his life, he became increasingly involved in the cocaine trade, smuggling about sixty tons of cocaine per year for the Colombians.

The drug lord established numerous contacts with Colombian drug traffickers, and he allowed them access to the same routes he used to ship heroin and marijuana into the U.S. from across the border at Chihuahua. Acosta Villarreal worked out a protection scheme with Mexican officials in which he secured the protection of the cocaine he smuggled every month from Colombia to his base at Ojinaga.

Carrillo Fuentes became not only a close associate of Acosta Villarreal, but also his best buddy. According to sources, they snorted cocaine together and rode together on drug smuggling trips. Acosta Villarreal, moreover, taught Amado how to move drugs, corrupt government officials and figure out whom to trust.

According to Terrance Poppa, the author of *Drug Lord: The Life and Death of a Mexican Drug Kingpin: A True Story*, "Carrillo learned from Pablo Acosta's failures. It was clear to him that a high profile led to his predecessor's end. This kept Carrillo in the shadows, expanding his influence quietly, building up his Guadalajara and Ojinaga connections, and on his relationship with his jailed uncle, Ernesto Fonseca Carrillo. He underwent periodic surgery to alter his appearance."

Pablo came to trust Amado like a son, and it cost him dearly. In April 1987, the Mexican authorities surrounded Pablo's ranch in Santa Elena, located just across the Rio Grande River from Big Bend National Park, and after a ninety-minute shootout, Acosta Villarreal was cut down in a hail of bullets.

Amado was not at Pablo's ranch when the raid took place, but American officials believe he had set up his boss and mentor by paying Guillermo González-Calderini, one of the highest commanders in the Mexican federal police, $1 million to kill him. Carrillo Fuentes and the commander continued to have a profitable relationship until 1992 when González-Calderini quit the police and left México because of indictments charging him with corruption.

Meanwhile, with his mentor out of the way, the ruthless and ambitious Amada Carrillo Fuentes could now focus on becoming Lord of the Skies.

ꕥ ꕥ

CHAPTER - 2

THE COLOMBIAN CONNECTION

Carrillo Fuentes did not miss a beat when it came to his relationship with the Colombian connection, the source of cocaine that Acosta Villarreal had assiduously trafficked. As part of his training under Pablo, Amado had to work with the Colombians to cultivate them as a source of supply.

Carrillo Fuentes established a lucrative working relationship with two of most powerful drug organizations the world has ever seen: The Cali and Medellín cartels. Named after the Colombian city of Medellín (population 3 million), the capital of Antioquia province, the Medellín Cartel was the country's most powerful drug-trafficking organization from the mid-1970s to the late 1980s, when it was crippled by the massive manhunt for its godfather, Pablo Escobar Gaviria, and the narco terrorist that he launched against the Colombian state. The cartel kept a high profile in its approach to drug trafficking, and in addition to Escobar, it included a number of godfathers or capos who became world famous and fabulously wealthy in the 1980s: José Rodríguez Gacha, Carlos Lehder and the Ochoa brothers (Jorge, Fabio, and Juan David).

Despite its brilliance in organizing the cocaine trade, the Medellín Cartel's emphasis on violence and narco terrorism to fulfill its criminal objectives ultimately led to its decline and fall. From 1984 to 1993 the cartel engaged the Colombian state in a war of attrition, which it ultimately lost. Medellín's dominance of the cocaine trade ended with the Colombian police killing Pablo Escobar in 1993 in a spectacular shoot out on a rooftop in Medellín.

Another Colombian gangster, Alberto Ochoa-Soto, a major money broker and one of the Medellín Cartel's highest ranking members, was among the first Colombians to work with Carrillo Fuentes. Ochoa-Soto first came to México in 1984 to oversee cocaine shipments coming from Colombia. In his frequent travels to Ojinaga, Ochoa-Soto met Carrillo Fuentes, and they became friends. Ochoa-Soto began collaborating with Carrillo Fuentes, and the two maintained close ties as Amado's organization grew in power and Carrillo Fuentes became the "premier patron" (boss) in México.

On July 9, 1994, the DEA arrested Ochoa-Soto for conspiracy to distribute six tons of cocaine. But despite the strong evidence, U.S. authorities released him from their custody on February 11, 1995.

Ochoa-Soto walked across the Stanton Street Bridge in El Paso and was never seen again. According to a DEA intelligence report, "recent reporting indicates that ACF (Amado Carrillo Fuentes) may have had Ochoa-Soto killed shortly after he returned to México because Ochoa-Soto was moving large quantities of cocaine through Ciudad Juárez without coordinating the movements with Carrillo Fuentes."

Carrillo Fuentes denied he had anything to do with Ochoa-Soto's death and claimed Ochoa-Soto fled with the cocaine. Interestingly, Carrillo Fuentes had the boldness of mind to think he could safely keep the twenty-two-ton shipment of cocaine worth $3 billion left after Ochoa's disappearance without experiencing any reprisals.

The Lord of the Skies was right. The Medellín Cartel seemed willing to forget the matter. Fabio Ochoa-Vasquez, one of the three brothers, who, with the death of Pablo Escobar took over the leadership of the Medellín Cartel, sent a conciliatory note to Carrillo Fuentes in which he said:

"What has happened, happened... We feel for our uncle's untimely death. Perhaps it was bad luck, perhaps it wasn't. In any case, we're not interested in revenge."

The Ochoas indicated that they wanted to continue doing business with Carrillo Fuentes. A source close to the Ochoas, however, later revealed that, privately, the Ochoas were furious and just biding their time, waiting for the right moment to exact sweet revenge.

Did that opportunity arise? Interestingly, two of the doctors who performed cosmetic surgery on Carrillo-Fuentes in 1997 in México City when the drug lord met his maker were Colombians.

Hoover Salazar-Espinosa, an important Cali Cartel transportation coordinator and money launderer, was an important and close Carrillo-Fuentes associate who helped cement the drug lord's relationship with the Cali Cartel. The Lord of the Skies provided protection for cocaine shipments that Salazar-Espinosa brokered and transported, and even helped to move the cocaine to crossing points along the U.S.-Mexican border and across the border with the assistance of Mexican crime federation members.

Once the cocaine was in the U.S., Salazar-Espinosa assumed control of the shipment and continued moving it to its destination. According to DEA intelligence, this scenario "showed ACF's (Amado Carrillo Fuentes) power and the flexibility of the Mexican drug trafficking alliances. With ACF's approval and protection, Salazar-Espinosa has the ability to smuggle and stage drugs along the entire length of the United States-Mexican border."

Carrillo Fuentes established a close working relationship with one particular powerful Colombian patron: Miguel Rodríguez Orejuela, a co-founder of the Cali Cartel. The Cali Cartel emerged in the late 1980s after the Medellín Cartel engaged the Colombian government in a bitter war of attrition and lost the power struggle. The Cali Cartel filled the vacuum and began supplying most of cocaine consumed in the United States and Europe.

Miguel Rodríguez and Amado Carrillo Fuentes reportedly talked about business almost every day. Rodríguez paid Amado a "transportation charge" of one kilo for every two kilos of Colombian cocaine that the Lord of the Skies successfully delivered to the United States.

Despite their close relationship, the two bosses constantly haggled over money, largely because Carrillo Fuentes was chronically overdue on his payments for the cocaine he bought from Miguel. Once Carrillo Fuentes had to send three Mexican hostages to Miguel as a guarantee that he would pay him for a lost shipment. The Mexicans were freed after Carrillo Fuentes paid Miguel millions of dollars and turned over some property in México to him.

Carrillo Fuentes learned well from the Cali Cartel. For one thing, he adopted the Cali Cartel's use of high-tech gadgetry, including beepers, fax machines, cell phones and encryption, as well as its terrorist-like cell structure, which compartmentalized each of the organization's functions.

"Amado Carrillo-Fuentes learned from the Cali bosses," said Tracey Eaton, a former México City bureau chief of the *Dallas Morning News* who has written extensively about Carrillo Fuentes. "He ran his operation much like a corporation and got into profit sharing before it was fashionable. He bribed Mexican police chiefs and politicians. He also had the touch of Tony Soprano, the star of the HBO TV series, *The Sopranos*, in that he could go from a polite gentleman to a ruthless thug in a minute."

Carrillo Fuentes' relationship with the Colombian connection did not suffer when Miguel Rodriguez Orejuela was arrested in August 1995. The Colombians valued their relationship with Amado Carrillo, and the Cali Cartel's Boeing 727 continued to land on the drug lord's Mexican airstrips.

Carrillo Fuentes was always looking for opportunities to expand his drug trafficking business, even in a country like Colombia where powerful associates operated and did not like foreign gangsters intruding on their space. Carrillo Fuentes allowed Grupo Union, a Mexican money laundering group, to operate in his area, and, reportedly, some of its members journeyed to Colombia to coordinate the arrival of aircraft on their ranches in the Mexican State of Tabasco. The Group then used Mexican rental vehicles to transport the cocaine across the U.S.-Mexican border. The traffickers sealed the powder in plastic and sprayed it with butane gas to mask the odor from cocaine detection devices.

☙ ❧

CHAPTER - 3

TAKING OVER

With Acosta García out of the way, Amado Carrillo Fuentes was closer to realizing his ambition to head the Juárez Cartel, control the Mexican drug trade and become México's most powerful player. The only drug trafficker who stood between Carrillo Fuentes and his goal was his new boss, Rafael Aguilar Guajardo, a one-time federal police commissioner of México's National Security and Investigation Center (CISEN).

Suspicion arose in drug trafficking circles that Aguilar Guajardo could be a snitch. The drug lord was suspected of cooperating with U.S. agents on the big bust at Sylmar, California, where, on September 29, 1989, U.S. authorities seized a warehouse and confiscated a staggering 21.4 tons of cocaine and $10 million in cash. At the time, it was described as the biggest drug bust in U.S. history.

According to Terrance Poppa, the author of *Drug Lord: The Life and Death of a Mexican Kingpin: A True Story*, "U.S. intelligence picked up information that Aguilar Guajardo had been complaining about the money he was being forced to pay (for protection from arrest). He threatened to go public with information about the Who's Who of Protection in México if he was not left alone.

On April 12, 1993, gunmen murdered the 43-year old Aguilar Guajardo at a Cancun, México, resort where he was vacationing with his family. A Colorado woman, who apparently was walking by at the time of the shooting, was caught in the crossfire and gunned down. Police arrested three gunmen who tried to flee by car on a highway headed out of Cancun. One of the suspects carried police credentials from the State of Morelos.

It was widely suspected that Carrillo Fuentes did the hit on Aguilar Guajardo for the Mexican authorities involved in protection schemes that Aguilar Guajardo had complained about.

The Mexican government seized Aguilar Guajardo assets, estimated to be more than $100 million. They included houses, nightclubs and a large chunk of property in Acapulco containing a luxury vacation home with 20 suites, salt water and fresh water swimming pools and a dock with two, 60-foot yachts.

With Aguilar Guajardo out of the way, Carrillo Fuentes was now the undisputed boss of the Juárez Cartel. To help him run his business, Carrillo Fuentes brought in his brother, Vicente Carrillo Fuentes, aka *The Viceroy* and *The General*.

The take down of the Medellín and Cali cartels gave Carrillo Fuentes the opportunity to take over cocaine distribution from the Colombians. Carrillo Fuentes upped his fees, now demanding from the Colombians about half of what they smuggled across the border as payment. The Carrillo Fuentes brothers, along with other Mexican drug kingpins, now set up their own independent distribution networks to transport cocaine, heroin, marijuana and methamphetamine into the U.S. This allowed them to expand their opportunities and become much more powerful.

Carrillo Fuentes also began carving out his own U.S. markets on the West Coast, the Southwest and in parts of the Midwest. At the apex of his power, Carrillo Fuentes was planning to expand his operation into the traditional Colombia strongholds on the U.S.'s East Coast, while cutting out the middle man in Columbia and expanding his drug business to countries as far away as Australia.

Carrillo Fuentes worked to unite the leaders of the Mexican cartels and brokered drug deals with the Colombians. He moved drugs by air and via fishing boats and pleasure crafts, through tunnels along the border and across border crossings via U.S. cargo trucks.

The Carrillo Fuentes organization used all kinds of innovative practices to smuggle drugs. For example, it outfitted its tractor trailers with sliding compartments in the roof to conceal the contraband. To divert suspicion, drivers who did not look Mexican were hired. Carrillo Fuentes compartmentalized the smugglers, truckers, warehouse crews and his other workers so that if someone was arrested, the others would not be snared.

Like his Colombian associates, Carrillo Fuentes was sophisticated in his use of technology and counter surveillance methods, and his network used state of the art communications devices to conduct business. The drug lord was an early pioneer in the use of cellphones when they became available in México. He acquired sophisticated scanners that allowed him to pirate frequencies and avoid surveillance.

Indeed, Amado Carrillo's use of technology could make James Bond envious. The drug lord owned a Dodge Ram pickup that came equipped with armored plating. When Carrillo Fuentes or an associate flicked on a switch at the bottom of the dashboard, the cab quickly filled up with smoke. The truck also had a mechanism that could create an oil slick behind the vehicle or deploy a canister that was filled up with shrapnel. Solid rubber tires prevented bullet-induced blowouts.

Carrillo Fuentes also focused on the human element. He compromised law enforcement officials on either side of the border, offering them a deal they couldn't refuse: the bullet or the bribe. But as one American law enforcement official noted, "The sheer number of vehicles coming across the border explain the success of the drug lords more than corruption would. Yes, corruption may be there. But how much is even needed?"

Carrillo was as ruthless as he was strategic, and his associates knew they would pay dearly if they screwed up a drug delivery. As one U.S. official explained, "He (Carrillo Fuentes) immediately ordered the assassination of everyone who could have turned the shipment in, and the bodies fall left and right."

Even being suspected of betrayal could mean a death sentence, for Carrillo Fuentes would have anyone suspected of being an informant killed, whether there was evidence or not. And he would get away with it, too. During one three-year period in Juárez, the Lord of the Skies' power base, there were 200 to 400 drug-related homicides. No one, least of all Carrillo Fuentes, was ever arrested.

As Carrillo Fuentes grew his drug smuggling organization, its reach became staggering. He regularly sent $20 to $30 million to Colombia to fund a drug smuggling operation, and as payoff, his criminal activities would generate tens of millions of dollars per week. His organization was so large that he needed three regular bases in Guadalajara, Hermosillo and Torreón to serve as strategic locations from which drugs could be moved closer to the U.S.-Mexican border for eventual shipment to the U.S.

U.S. authorities busted several of Carrillo Fuentes' drug smuggling operations, but all the busts did was show the remarkable extent of his organization. In one bust alone, an investigation known as *Operation Limelight* revealed that the Carrillo Fuentes organization was smuggling 1.5 tons of cocaine a month in cartons of fruits and vegetables from México.

In March 1997, a New York drug task force confiscated 3,600 pounds of cocaine buried in a shipment of carrots packed in a truck near La Guardia Airport in New York City. Nine suspects were arrested and $1.3 million in cash seized.

On June 11, 1997, drug agents found another 1,350 pounds of cocaine hidden inside a stack of plywood in a warehouse in Jersey City. According to one agent who was there, "The plywood was hollowed out like a coffin inside, and all the coke was there."

On December 3, 1997, U.S. authorities found another 5.3 tons of cocaine stashed in a warehouse in Tucson, Arizona. Soon after, law enforcement agents seized 1.5 tons of cocaine in El Paso. And then from one truck heading to New York City, law enforcement seized 2,700 pounds of marijuana and $2 million in cash from another truck returning from New York.

And the hits just kept coming. Between December 1996 and August 1997, U.S. federal agents seized more than three tons of cocaine, seven tons of marijuana and more than $18 million in drug profits from busts in several U.S. cities, including New York City, Chicago and Los Angeles.

With his wealth, power and connections, Carrillo Fuentes turned Ciudad Juárez virtually into a company town. "They're (México) not investigating Carrillo Fuentes," explained one disgusted U.S. official. "We are, but they're not. It's a shame that the citizens of Juárez are under siege by his (Carrillo Fuentes) group and nothing is being done."

U.S. drug officials worried about the spillover effect of Ciudad Juárez's drug culture on the neighboring U.S. city of El Paso. "One day we're going to wake up and realize that much of the economy of El Paso is reliant on drug money," Tom Kennedy, an assistant special agent in charge of the DEA's El Paso office, told the *Texas Monthly* magazine in December 1995. "If we're ever successful at putting away Carrillo Fuentes and shutting down the drug traffic here, numerous businesses in this city will crash and burn. El Paso is not a big city like Miami; it won't be able to absorb the impact. It will be like a cancer... something we can't find and can't diagnose until we experience the sudden pain. And then it will be too late."

Carrillo was having a big impact on the U.S., but, unlike other Mexican drug lords, he was not curious himself to find out what was going on north of the border. As far as we know, he never crossed the border to visit and party.

The Lord of the Skies could have lived anywhere, but he chose to make his home village of Guamuchulito his base. He lived in a surprisingly modest one-story building on grounds that did not even contain a swimming pool. But the expensive Lincoln Town Cars, Chevy station wagons and Dodge pickups parked on the property hinted at Carrillo Fuentes' wealth.

El Hombre, as the drug lord liked to be called, could be seen strolling the streets of his hometown with his bodyguards. He liked to mix with community, and locales would prepare his favorite foods for him, particularly stuffed chili peppers and a stew made from pork belly.

When reporters came to Guamuchulito to find information about Carrillo Fuentes, the locales beamed with pride at the mere mention of his name. One local resident, Guadalupe García, told a reporter that Carrillo Fuentes "is a good man, not at all like you say he is. If it wasn't for him, we would not have our church." Another local resident described the drug lord and his family as "good, quiet Christian people, just like anyone else here."

Many of the townsfolk recalled Amado as quiet and hard working. One resident told an American reporter about how "Amado would take care of his parents," and "how he often tended the chickens... He sure liked to milk cows," the resident recalled. "He did it very fast. And he liked to drink milk, too. Sometimes he would drink milk right from the udder."

Carrillo Fuentes helped the poor in his hometown. For instance, he built a modest church and a basketball court for the kids. He was also generous towards his workers, giving them a Christmas bonus each year. But he was no Pablo Escobar of Colombia's Medellín Cartel fame, who built houses and a community, the so-called Medellín without Slums, for the poor. Still, Guamuchulito revered the Lord of the Skies as its favorite son.

ଔ ଓ

PHOTOS

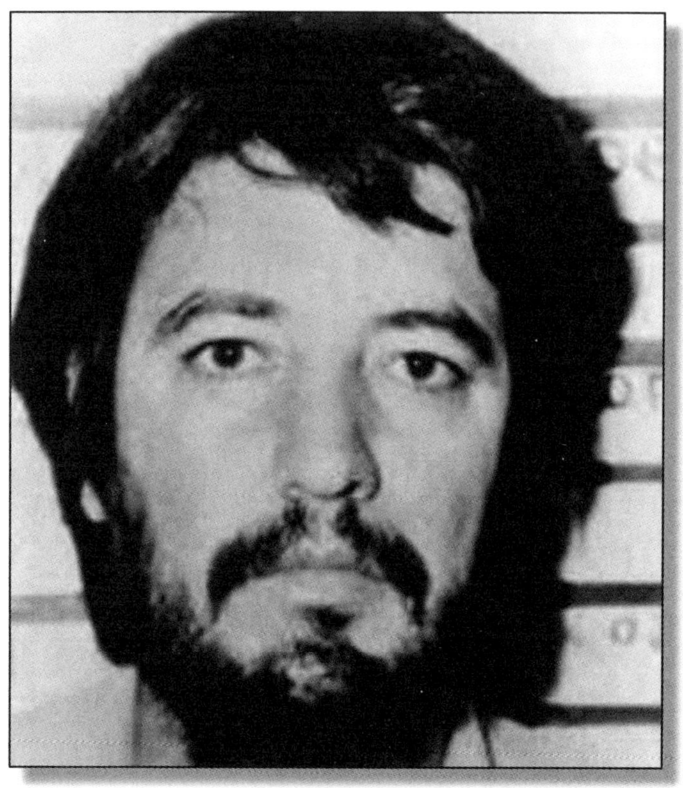

Amado Carrillo Fuentes
also known as
"El Señor de los Cielos"
"Lord of the Skies"

Juan Abrego

Pablo Acosta Villarreal
"El Zorro de Ojinaga"

General José de Jesús Gutiérrez Rebollo

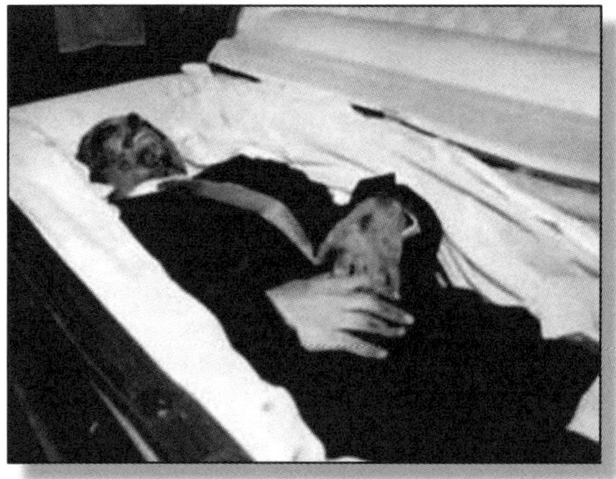

Amado Carrillo Fuentes
Dead after botched plastic surgery

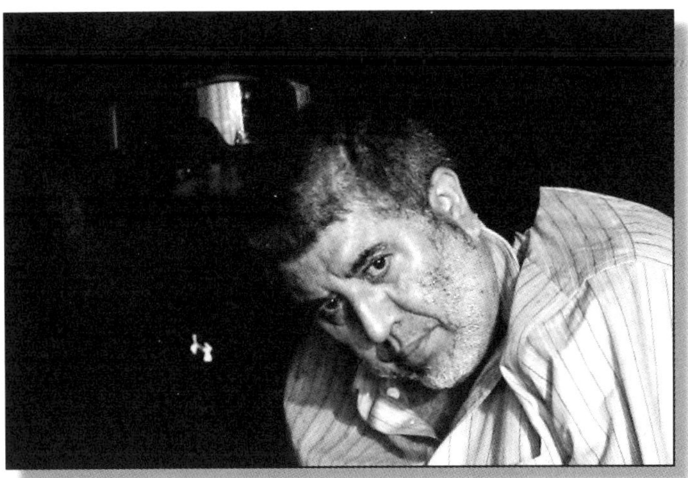

Vicente Carrillo Fuentes
(brother)

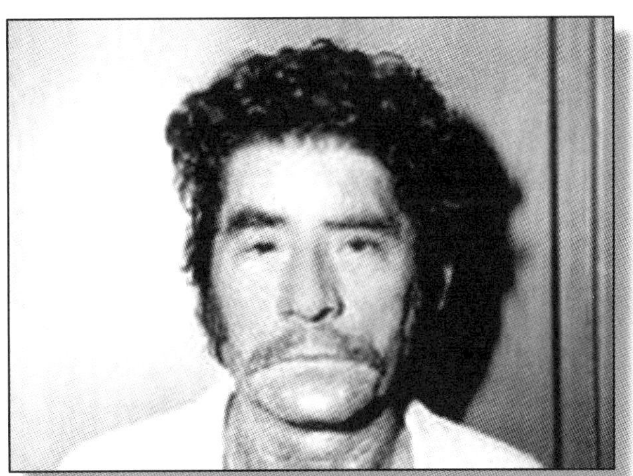

Ernesto Fonseca Carrillo
(uncle)

Vicente Carrillo Leyva
(son)

Rafael Caro Quintero
Founder of the Guadalajara Cartel

ઙ ઙ

CHAPTER - 4

OWNING MEXICO

Despite his growing prominence as the notorious Lord of the Skies, Carrillo Fuentes was untouchable. Even when the U.S. government tried to get Carrillo Fuentes extradited on drug trafficking charges, it was to no avail.

He was arrested just one time over the course of his drug smuggling career—by Guadalajara police in July 1989. Fingerprinted and jailed, he was supposed to go to trial, but nine months later, he was set free, never to be seriously in trouble again—that is, until 1996, when, with the arrest of Juan Abrego García, the drug lord became México's most wanted man.

Still, even with this close brush with the law, Carrillo Fuentes didn't miss a beat. Indeed, Mexican authorities began calling him the "Lord of the Heavens."

The drug lord was able to protect his growing criminal empire because he could corrupt powerful individuals at the highest echelons of the Mexican establishment and get away with it. Corruption did not come cheap. It is estimated that Carrillo Fuentes had to pay between $500 to $800 million yearly in bribes. Still, it was money well spent.

A 1994 DEA intelligence report graphically detailed how Carrillo Fuentes did it. According to the report, the drug lord "purchased influence at various levels of the Mexican government, and by establishing powerful connections he ensured safe passage of his illegal drug shipments through México to the U.S."

The close ties between Carrillo Fuentes and the Mexican establishment were revealed in a scandal involving a bank and powerful interests in the Mexican financial system. In 1995 several front men acting on behalf of Carrillo Fuentes offered to invest several million dollars in Grupo Financiero Anahuac, a troubled México City bank. For sinking $12.6 million into the bank, Carrillo Fuentes was given an ownership position, which he used to launder his drug profits and send nearly $30 million through the bank to secret bank accounts in the Cayman Islands.

He did this for two years until 1996 when one of the bank's big shareholders was implicated in a separate fraud not related to narcotics, and the Mexican government discovered the ploy. The government seized the bank and froze the accounts of Carrillo Fuentes.

The scandal eventually entangled the brother of President Ernesto Zedillo, as well as the son and the nephew of a former presidential candidate and the head of México's labor confederation. Only by luck were the Mexican authorities able to thwart Carrillo Fuentes' desire to control the bank.

Carlos Salinas de Gortari served as President of México from 1988 to 1994, but many suspected that his 1988 election to the presidency was rigged and that perhaps Cuauhtémoc Cárdenas of the Party of the Democratic Revolution (PRD) was the true winner. While no smoking gun was every found, many in México believed Salinas had a direct link to Fuentes Carrillo. One source claimed he saw Salinas and Carrillo Fuentes together in 1989. Eduardo Valle, a former adviser to México's attorney general during the Salinas administration, claimed he had to flee México for his life after he uncovered narco links with the Mexican government.

Salinas' family had strong links to drug trafficking. In January 1992, for example, Carlos Enrique Cervantes de Gortari, the cousin of President Carlos Salinas, was convicted of drug trafficking in a U.S. court and sentenced to fifteen years in prison. The following year, the Mexican press published a document suggesting that Raúl Salinas, President Salinas' brother, was present at a meeting in which drug traffickers made payoffs to Mexican anti-drug officials. Carrillo Fuentes was reported to be at one of these meetings.

Later, in February 1995, Raúl was arrested for his alleged involvement in the 1994 killing of José Francisco Ruiz Massieu, who was about to become the leader of México's opposition PRI party. In January 1999, Raúl Salinas was found guilty and sentenced to 50 years in prison (later reduced to 27.5 years). Raúl Salinas' sentence was overturned in 2005.

Carlos Salinas did his best to impede U.S. anti-drug enforcement efforts in México. In 1992, for instance, he imposed the first written regulations on DEA agents, which included limiting the number of agents who could operate in México, designating certain areas in which they had to live, denying U.S. officials diplomatic immunity, requiring that all information collected by the U.S. government be turned over to Mexican authorities and prohibiting DEA agents operating in México from carrying guns.

When President Ernesto Zedillo prepared to take office on December 1, 1994, as Carlos Salinas' successor, he asked the American government for a list of the names of officials whom Uncle Sam suspected of having ties to drug traffickers. One former U.S. official recalled, "The Zedillo administration wanted the names of people believed to be corrupt, or possibly in the pay of traffickers, whom the United States would not like to see in the new government."

Two of the names belonged to governors Manlo Fabio Beltrones Rivera and Jorge Carrillo Olea. But while neither governor was offered a post in the Zedillo government, neither were they investigated for corruption.

As the cases of these two governors showed, the corruption in México extended all the way from the President's office down to the local state level. In 1997 *The New York Times* reported that Beltrones Rivera and Carrillo Olea had participated in meetings in which Carrillo Fuentes and other prominent drug traffickers paid bribes to leading Mexican politicians to protect their operations.

American officials believed Carrillo Fuentes operated with impunity in the State of Sonora, which Beltrones governed, although Beltrones vehemently denied it. "These reports are incredible in every sense...filled with fantasies and lies," Beltrones angrily charged.

In an interview, Beltrones took the offensive, claiming he had virtually kicked Carrillo Fuentes out of his state. According to his spin, shortly after taking office as governor, Beltrones learned that Carrillo Fuentes was living in a city named Hermosillo. Beltrones said he ordered aides to videotape Carrillo Fuentes' arrival at the town's airport and his subsequent movements. The governor claimed he gave the tapes to President Carlos Salinas, and that, as a result, federal authorities confiscated four of Carrillo Fuentes' properties.

"How would the DEA explain that I'm the one who took away this man's (Carrillo Fuentes) houses?" Beltrones asked one interviewer.

The DEA acknowledged that the four properties owned by Carrillo Fuentes were seized, but the agency pointed out that the drug lord still had eight properties in the town, which he continued to use. Sonora State continued to be among the most important of Carrillo Fuentes' operating bases.

The Mexican political establishment served Carrillo Fuentes well as he expanded his air smuggling operations. Jorge Carrillo Olea (not related to Amado) a former army general, was appointed head of a drug intelligence center that used a radar system to track aircraft flying into México from Colombia. According to one intelligence report, "From about 1992, indications are that the former Mexican coordinator against narcotic trafficking, Jorge Carrillo Olea, was at the time Amado Carrillo Fuentes' most influential associate in the Mexican government. Carrillo Olea was in charge of controlling the radar detection in México, and by utilizing the information provided to him, he was able to ensure safe passage of Carrillo Fuentes aircraft."

In January 1996, Mexican authorities raided a ranch in Sinaloa during a wedding reception for Carrillo Fuentes' sister, hoping to capture him; but tipped off, the drug lord stayed away. Commanding the failed raid was General José de Jesús Gutiérrez Rebollo, the national anti-drug coordinator and a 42-year career military man. A year later, the good general was arrested and accused of being on Carrillo Fuentes' payroll for seven years, even as he served as a commander in México's anti-drug program.

Imagine if the most powerful drug kingpin in the U.S formed an alliance with the most important anti-drug official in the U.S., the so called drug czar. That's what happened in México, and it represented one of the most egregious examples of corruption in Mexican history. Carrillo Fuentes, of course, was the drug lord, and the drug czar was General José de Jesús Gutiérrez Rebollo.

Gutiérrez Rebollo was born on April 19, 1934, in the town of Jonacatepec in the Mexican state of Morelos. He served in numerous regional coordinator positions until he reached the top of the military hierarchy. He commanded the fifth military region, which was based in Jalisco, and there he worked for the Office of the Attorney General.

In 1996 he was appointed the head of the Instituto Nacional Para el Combate a Las Drogas (NCD), making him the country's top-ranking drug interdiction officer. He had access to all kinds of intelligence that the U.S. provided to México, including anti-drug investigations, wiretaps, interdiction programs and operations and informant information.

Gutiérrez Rebollo operated in a sea of corruption, but he was the Mexican official with whom U.S. government bureaucrats under President Bill Clinton wanted to work. General Barry McCaffrey, the U.S. anti-drug czar, praised Gutiérrez Rebollo as "a soldier of absolute unquestioned integrity." The U.S. government trusted the general to the point where he was invited to Washington for briefings.

Gutiérrez Rebollo looked like the poster boy for the career officer who had diligently worked his way up from the bottom. Instead, he became the model for the corrupt general in director Steven Soderbergh's 2000 movie, "Traffic."

It is believed Carrillo Fuentes' relationship with Gutiérrez Rebollo began in 1996 when the drug lord's top lieutenant, Eduardo González Quirarte, a Guadalajara businessman, contacted General Gutiérrez Rebollo and established a relationship.

The Mexican authorities began investigating the general on February 6, 1997, when they received a tip that he had moved into an expensive apartment whose rent could not have possibly been paid for by the wages received by someone working as a public servant.

Then came the smoking gun. Mexican authorities obtained a recording of Gutiérrez Rebollo and Carrillo Fuentes discussing payments to be made to the general in return for the general agreeing to ignore Fuentes' drug smuggling activities.

On February 19, 1997, Enrique Cervantes, the Mexican defense minister, held a news conference where he publicly accused Gutiérrez Rebollo of using his authority to help protect Carrillo Fuentes. According to reports, when confronted with the evidence, the general collapsed from what appeared to be a heart attack.

Gutiérrez Rebollo was soon fired from his job, taken into custody and charged with bribery, drug trafficking and aiding Carrillo Fuentes in his illicit activities. Rumors circulated that after the general's arrest and hospitalization, the Mexican military had planned to kill him and then announce he had died of diabetes or heart trouble.

Gutiérrez Rebollo's lawyer, Arturo González Vásquez, presented a vigorous defense of the general, portraying his client's arrest as part of a big power struggle within the military in which some of the top military commanders were collaborating with trafficking groups based in Tijuana and Ciudad Juárez. Arturo González received death threats, and the Mexican government was accused of trying to get him to resign from the Gutiérrez Rebollo defense team.

In April 1998, González was found dead in his car. He had been shot to death with a .9-millimeter pistol.

Gutiérrez Rebollo took the stand and claimed he had tried to arrest Carrillo Fuentes. As an example, he used the raid of the wedding reception for Carrillo Fuentes' sister in the State of Sinaloa. According to the general, the drug lord had been tipped off and fled.

An examination of the general's record, however, revealed a stark pattern that showed how the general had pursued some drug trafficking groups aggressively but had carefully stayed away from Carrillo Fuentes. The authorities learned that to help protect Gutiérrez Rebollo, Carrillo Fuentes provided him with armored cars and encrypted cell phones.

Gutiérrez Rebollo sang like the proverbial canary. He also testified that drug traffickers, including Carrillo Fuentes, met several times with Mexican military officials. The Mexican military acknowledged that such a meeting took place, but insisted that the officers who attended did not know they were meeting with drug traffickers. "The claim that there were any other meetings is false," a top aide to the Mexican Defense Minister said in a press interview. The aide further claimed that the allegations represented a bold face attempt by Gutiérrez Rebollo to save himself by implicating others; in other words, snitching.

As part of the investigation of Gutiérrez Rebollo, the authorities went looking for Luis Octavio López Vega, who had worked closely with the Mexican military and the DEA as a senior advisor to Gutiérrez Rebollo. The Mexicans wanted him, too, as a prime suspect in the case, but the Americans found him first. In exchange for his cooperation, the DEA hustled López across the U.S.–Mexican border. After dozens of hours of testimony, Lopez convincingly established the corrupt connection between Mexican drugs cartels and the country's military.

Gutiérrez Rebollo was sentenced to 31 years, 10 months and 15 days in prison. Ten years later, he was sentenced by a Mexican federal court to an additional forty years in prison.

It was one of México's most spectacular falls from political grace. It ended on December 19, 2013, when the general died of brain cancer at a military hospital in México City.

CHAPTER - 5

DEATH

At the beginning of 1997, Carrillo Fuentes was on top of the world, but his increasing notoriety and the revelations about his connection to government corruption had sown the seeds of his own destruction. Carrillo Fuentes was aware that the Mexican authorities were now tracking him more closely than they had in the past. The Zedillo government was under intense pressure, given the shocking arrest of Jesús Gutiérrez Rebollo, the man in charge of México's anti-drug policy. This scandal, along with the move in U.S. Congress to decertify México as an ally in the War on Drugs, put tremendous pressure on Mexican President Zedillo to do something about the Lord of the Skies.

In anticipation of what was to come, Carrillo Fuentes began looking for a way to save himself, his family and his fortune. In the months before his death, Carrillo Fuentes rarely saw his family or spent the night in the same place twice, as he tried to stay one step ahead of his pursuers.

According to Edward Fallis, a DEA agent who investigated the Carrillo Fuentes organization , "Knowing how close we were to getting an indictment that could lead to his extradition, Amado began to take dramatic, evasive measures—much like Pablo Escobar and other Colombia drug lords had done earlier when under threat of extradition to the United States."

In his memoir, *The Dark Art: My Undercover Life in Global Narcoterrorism*, Fallis revealed that Carrillo Fuentes went on a secret tour in search of a place to stash his billions. According to Fallis, Carrillo Fuentes became so paranoid about being caught that he would only move around Ciudad Juárez in ambulances—no ordinary ambulances, but ambulances that had interiors as opulent as those found in the drug lord's regular means of transportation.

On July 14, 1997, Carrillo Fuentes' top aide, Eduardo González Quirarte, met with several Mexican generals to negotiate a way out of the drug trade for Carrillo Fuentes. Accounts of that meeting differ substantially. According to the generals who participated, the offer was rejected.

But Carrillo Fuentes and many observers begged to differ. According to their spin, the generals accepted a $5 million bribe, and then reneged on the deal.

Carrillo Fuentes made other proposals to the Mexican government. He offered to collaborate with the Mexican government and help to take down other drug traffickers. The drug lord said he could help the Mexican economy by stopping the sale of drugs in the country and selling them instead to the U.S. and to countries in Europe.

Carrillo became desperate. He sent his family to Chile and moved to the Cayman Islands, but returned to México City in July 1997, where he had more plastic surgery to keep the authorities off his trail.

Determined to make himself unrecognizable, the drug lord checked into the Santa Monica hospital in the upscale Polanco district of México City under a false name. With the drug lord was his usual bodyguards as well as two doctors from his native Sinaloa and a third doctor from Colombia. Carrillo Fuentes went under the knife in an eight-and-a half hour operation that included liposuction of the thorax. The doctors removed 30 pounds of fat from Carrillo Fuentes' body, changed the shape of his eyes and nose, broke his lower jaw and inserted a prosthesis to alter his jaw line.

The operation, however, went terribly wrong, and Carrillo Fuentes died on the operating table. It took a week and DNA testing before the authorities conclusively determined that the body with the black and blue facial bruises belonged to Carrillo Fuentes.

What had gone wrong? Some sources speculated that Carrillo Fuentes' drug use was to blame. Pathologists did find indicators of drug abuse, such as an absence of nose hairs. Other sources believed the operation had put a strain on his heart, already weakened by cocaine use, and that killed him. The official report of Carrillo Fuentes' death stated that he died because too much anesthetics were applied during the operation. A nurse and other hospital personnel present during the operation reported that an "unknown doctor" had entered the operating room several times and then vanished.

Mariano Herrán Salvatti, head of México's anti-drug agency, told the press: "We have concluded that acting with malice and with the intention of taking his (Carrillo Fuentes) life, these physicians supplied a combination of medicines that resulted in the death of the trafficker." On November 7, 1997, five days after Carrillo Fuentes' death, Mexican authorities issued arrest warrants for the three doctors who performed the operation.

The mutilated corpses of two of the physicians who had operated on the Lord of the Skies were found in concrete barrels beside a highway. The bodies showed signs of torture, and the victims had been gagged and encased in 66-gallon oil drums. The victims' fingernails were ripped out and the bodies covered with burn marks. One had been shot and strangled, with cables still wrapped around his neck. Another mangled body found in a similar barrel of concrete was believed to belong to the third doctor who had helped with the surgery.

The speculation as to how the Lord of the Skies died knew no bounds. One television program claimed that the drug lord was smothered with a pillow, while certain press reports favored the idea of a drug overdose. Some observers believed that the Lord of the Skies had faked his own death. Other bizarre conspiracy theories abounded. For instance, Carrillo Fuentes was actually in the U.S. Federal Witness Protection Program, and one of Carrillo Fuentes' own bodyguards had murdered the drug lord during the operation.

A Chilean newspaper even reported that Carrillo Fuentes was alive and cooperating with Mexican anti-drug officials. The DEA was quick to respond with a terse statement that read: "The rumor has as much credibility as the millions of sightings of the late Elvis Presley."

One resident of Carrillo Fuentes' home town summed up the feeling about the mystery of Carrillo Fuentes' death: "Nobody knows if he's dead but his mom. He could buy a whole country if he wanted to."

Amado's mother identified the corpse in the México City morgue as her son. "Yes, it's my son," she told reporters.

In November 1997, more mystery was added to the Carrillo Fuentes saga when one of Carrillo Fuentes' lawyers went missing. He had missed a court date and relatives had not heard from him. The authorities opened a missing person's investigation.

The Lord of the Skies was mysterious while alive, but after his death Mexican, U.S. and Chilean law enforcement officials made a veritable flood of information available about him, much of which added to the on-going mystery. Among the revelations—Carrillo Fuentes had a second family in Chile, and he was a benefactor of the Catholic Church in México. He frequently traveled abroad to Europe, Turkey, Brazil, Ecuador, and Argentina, often on fake passports, for what reason, it was not known. In 1995 the newspapers published a photo of the drug lord with a Mexican priest in, of all places, Jerusalem in Israel.

Amidst all the mystery and controversy, Carrillo Fuentes got a huge send off at his family ranch, with more than 1,200 people attending services for the 41-year-old drug trafficker. The locals turned out as well in respect for the gangster they viewed as a hero.

People arrived in fancy cars, carrying floral wreaths, some six feet tall. Several mourners dressed like Mexican drug traffickers in Stetson hats and snakeskin cowboy boots. Dozens of soldiers and police kept an eye on the mourners and even frisked some of them.

Carrillo Fuentes' body lay in an open casket in the sweltering heat, surrounded by wilting funeral wreaths. One of the wreaths that arrived consisted entirely of black roses. A Carrillo Fuentes family member recalled: "After the funeral, when some of us were helping clean away the funeral wreaths, we couldn't help ourselves, and out of curiosity, we started reading the cards that accompanied the wreaths. Somebody noticed that one of the cards said: 'All good things come to those that know how to wait'. And near the bottom of the card, right before an illegible signature, [was] a greeting from the Ochoa family of Colombia."

ଓ ଛ

CHAPTER - 6

AFTERMATH

Amado Carrillo Fuentes' death created a large power vacuum in the Mexican underworld and put his organization in disarray. After engaging in a brief turf war in Juárez over the cartel's leadership, Vicente Carrillo Fuentes, Amado's brother, defeated the Muñoz Talavera brothers and gained control of the Juárez Cartel.

Vicente formed a partnership with Juan José Esparragoza Moreno, his brother Rodolfo Carrillo Fuentes, his nephew Vicente Carrillo Leyva (the son of Amado), Ricardo García Urquiza and the Beltrán Leyva brothers. As part of his organization, Vicente kept on the payroll several of the lieutenants who had worked for his brother Amado.

As the Carrillo Fuentes organization tottered along, it had to fight vicious gang battles to survive. From 2009 to 2011 in Ciudad Juárez, for instance, Vicente oversaw a brutal turf war with the rival Sinaloa Cartel that is believed to have killed more than 8,000 people.

According to a biography published by the Mexican newspaper *El Universal*, Carrillo Fuentes told his son, Carrillo Leyva, not to get involved with the drug trafficking business. Consistent with this desire, the father sent the son to study at the best private universities of México, Switzerland, and Spain. The son, however, paid no attention to his father.

Junior was arrested by Mexican police on April 2, 2009, as he jogged near his home in México City. Carrillo Leyva, whom the Mexican media described as being a part of a new generation of cartel bosses called "narco juniors," was subsequently acquitted of money laundering charges, though illegal possession of firearms charges kept him in jail. Found guilty of illegal arms possession, he paid a $16,000 fine and was released on December 17, 2010, to the custody of Mexican federal police. The Mexican government then filed new charges of money laundering.

The Carrillo Fuentes organization took a big blow in September 1999 when the U.S. government announced the conclusion of a two-year international investigation known as "Operation Impunity," a multi-jurisdictional, multi-agency complex investigation that culminated in the arrest of 93 individuals linked to the Carrillo Fuentes organization.

"The impact of *Operation Impunity* is significant," said U.S. Attorney General Janet Reno. "By targeting the cartel's importation, transportation and distribution network, we have substantially hindered their ability to move cocaine and other drugs into, and around, this country."

During the duration of *Operation Impunity*, Uncle Sam seized $19 million in U.S. currency, another $7 million in assets, and more than 12,434 kilos of cocaine and 4,800 lbs. of marijuana. Donnie Marshall, Acting Administrator of the Drug Enforcement Administration, stated that "this investigation graphically proves the reach and depth of the internationally directed cocaine trade that affects far too many communities within our nation—from major cities to smaller cities, from suburban locations to rural areas."

The investigation identified and arrested three major drug trafficking cell heads of the Carrillo Fuentes organization—individuals on the payroll of major drug lords who directed their operations within U.S. cities. They were Arturo Arredondo, aka "Aman", who was responsible for giving orders to traffickers based in the United States regarding all U.S. transportation and distribution activities; Jesse Quintanilla, aka "*Sobrino*", who was in charge of all Chicago distribution of cocaine from México; and Jorge Ontiveros-Rodríguez, aka "Guillermo Alfonso", who was the San Diego cell head responsible for cocaine distribution.

In 2004 Amado's brother, Rodolfo Carrillo Fuentes, was killed outside of a movie theatre allegedly at the behest of Joaquín Guzmán Loera, today the world's most famous drug trafficker. Born in Badiraguato, Sinaloa, either on December 25, 1954, or April 4, 1957, Guzmán, who became known as "El Chapo" (Shorty), began his drug trafficking career working for powerful drug lord Miguel Angel Félix Gallardo before founding his own cartel in 1980.

His drug empire, the Sinaloa Cartel, became México's most powerful. Guzmán surrounded himself with ruthless enforcers and reigned over a multibillion-dollar global drug empire that eventually supplied much of the marijuana, cocaine and heroin peddled on the streets of the U.S. When Joaquín Guzmán Loera escaped from prison in 2011, many of the Juárez Cartel members defected to Guzmán's Sinaloa Cartel.

Vicente Carrillo responded to the killing of Rodolfo by having El Chapo's brother "*El Pollo*" assassinated in prison. This sparked off a turf war, although it seemed that the war between the two was put on hold during 2005 and 2006 because the Sinaloa Cartel was engaged in a vicious war with their rival, the Gulf Cartel.

During this time, the leadership of the cartel was actually shared between Vicente Carrillo and Ricardo García Urquiza, but then he was arrested in November 2005. The Carrillo Fuentes organization cartel then became factionalized into two groups: one loyal to the Carrillo family and the other to the Sinaloa Cartel drug lord Juan José Esparragoza Moreno and Joaquín Guzmán Loera's Sinaloa Cartel.

The Juárez Cartel, under the control of Vicente Carrillo Fuentes and his nephew Vicente Carrillo Leyva, was placed under a large degree of pressure following the "House of Death" case, which refers to a serial killing site in the Mexican city of Ciudad Juárez. Executions were committed by members of the Juárez Cartel, some allegedly with the knowledge and participation of a United States undercover informant known by the pseudonym "*Lalo*" who had infiltrated the cartel. The fact that the informant participated in some of the murders corrupted investigation.

About 200 murders occurred in the first three months of 2008, and it appeared that the war between the Sinaloa Federation and the remnants of the Juárez Cartel was back on. President Calderón even had to send thousands of troops to Ciudad Juárez to quell the violence.

On October 19, 2014, México's military and federal police forces captured Vicente Carrillo Fuentes in the northern city of Torreon in Coahuila State following an 11-month investigation that identified a vehicle he used and two homes he'd visited. Besides dozens of charges in México, Vicente was also charged in U.S. federal court with murder, attempted murder, drug trafficking and money laundering. Even before a formal announcement of his arrest was made, the U.S. Drug Enforcement Administration issued a statement congratulating México and calling Vincent Carrillo Fuentes "one of history's most notorious drug traffickers."

The Juárez Cartel during the career of the Lord of the Skies was the most powerful in México. Today, it is a shadow of its former self. The Mexican drug trade has moved on, but nothing has changed, especially the violence and corruption that still permeates the country.

At this writing, *El Chapo* Guzmán, having escaped prison, has been recaptured and returned to *Altiplano*, the same prison from which he escaped last July. The U.S. Justice Department wants

Guzmán extradited, brought here to face charges for his crimes. Seven separate jurisdictions—including New York, Chicago and San Diego—all want to put *El Chapo* on trial.

El Chapo's exploits, power and wealth have made him a legend. Yet, it is Amado Carrillo Fuentes who is the first big-time Mexican drug lord and perhaps its most powerful drug trafficker. If México has its equivalent of Al *"Scarface"* Capone, it should be Amado Carrillo Fuentes, the *Lord of the Skies*.

Carrillo Fuentes died young, but criminally, he accomplished much. For one important thing, after the Colombian drug trade collapsed in the early to mid-1990s, he laid the groundwork for today's Mexican drug trade. We can only speculate how big the Lord of Skies would have been if he had lived.

☙ ❧ ☙ ❧

SHRIMP BOY

蝦男孩

The Life and Times of Raymond Chow, Chinatown Gangster

PROLOGUE

A MURDER IN CHINATOWN

To many in San Francisco's close-knit Chinese community, Allen Leung was an influential local leader and a successful business man, well known and respected. But in early 2006, the people of Chinatown were not aware that Leung was a man in fear for his life.

An examination of Leung's resume reveals much to admire about the man, and one might have wondered what the community leader had to fear. By all accounts, Leung was an American success story. In 1971, at age 20, he left Hong Kong for the San Francisco Bay Area with little money and in pursuit of the American Dream. Once he arrived, he never looked back.

The ambitious immigrant learned English and attended San Francisco State University where he graduated with a business degree and earned a real estate license. At the time, he was also working as a bilingual counselor at John O'Connell High School. Despite his many business interests and civic responsibilities, Leung still found the time to start a travel agency and then turn it into a thriving import-export business.

The more successful Leung became, the more his wealth grew, and he was able to buy houses not only in San Francisco but also in Las Vegas and Florida. Leung got involved with the community and immersed himself in civic affairs. He became a volunteer Taiwan commissioner for the U.S., the highest honorary position for overseas pro-Taiwan leaders, even though he had never lived in Taiwan.

According to friends and supporters, Leung was the "perfect" leader who was respectful to everyone, even if he disagreed with them. "Some people don't like him, but he treats them nicely," Bill Wong, another prominent Chinatown citizen, explained to the SFGate website. "He sometimes has a different opinion, but he always tries to compromise. You never hear him trying to do something in his own interests. He always thinks about the association (that Leung and Wong belonged to) and the Chinese community."

Leung projected a benevolent image, but he was no push-over. One night in April 1977, a burglar broke into his family home. Leung shot the intruder in the chest, killing him. Police ruled the shooting a justifiable homicide.

Yet, Leung had a mysterious side. Few people knew that he was a leader in a secretive Chinese Tong organization called Hip Sing Tong, where he was known as Dragon Head. The word Tong means meeting hall or gathering place. The Tongs were founded in 17th century Imperial China, and in America they can trace their beginnings to the California Gold Rush and the mid-19th century before they spread to other parts of the country.

In the U.S., the Tongs started off as a benevolent organization to help Chinese immigrants deal with discrimination, but according to U.S. authorities, the organization was already heavily under criminal influence by the time Leung became a member. Authorities suspected that the Tongs, including Hip Sing Tong, were into criminal activities like gambling, drugs, prostitution, and so-called "protection services," which amounted to extortion. The Tongs are like secretive societies or sworn brotherhoods and will affiliate with Chinese gangs, which they often control for their own protection.

In San Francisco, the Tongs became a powerful institution. “If you go and look at the history of Chinatown, the Tongs were always important,” Peter Huston, the author of *Tongs, Gangs and Triads: Chinese Crime Groups in North America,* told the Walnut Creek, California-based *Contra Costa Times*. “As more and more people came from Hong Kong, they brought their organizations with them. In about the 1970s, the modern day type of street gang started to become prominent.”

Yet, despite his influence and power, Leung lived in fear of certain younger members of his own Hip Sing Tong organization. Normally, the Chinese community does not deal with the local police because it has never really trusted the authorities. Leung, however, was in such fear that in March 2005 he approached the San Francisco Police Department for help.

Leung told the authorities that Raymond Chow, an ex-convict and gang associate, had demanded about $120,000 to start a so-called youth group. The FBI interviewed Chow about Leung’s claim, but Chow denied there was any extortion attempt.

The authorities, however, viewed Chow as one of the most prominent gangsters in San Francisco’s Chinatown. An early 1990s report of the U.S. Senate Permanent Subcommittee on Investigations had identified Chow as “a well-known source of muscle” in Asian organized crime in the San Francisco Bay Area and charged that “he had been allegedly involved in kidnapping and home invasion robberies and had been identified by law enforcement agencies as a critical player in Wo Hop To’s recent surge.” Wo Hop To is a Triad group based in Wanchai, Hong Kong.

In 2003, Chow was released from prison when his sentence was cut in half after he agreed to testify against an associate named Peter Chong. Chow was lucky. He should have been deported to Hong Kong.

After release, Chow tried to portray himself as a reformed man no longer involved in organized crime. He gave interviews in which he freely talked about his past. He worked with kids to keep them out of trouble. He even wrote an autobiography about his years in the Chinese underworld, which he claimed were behind him.

Chow liked to tell anyone who would listen that he was no longer in organized crime and that he was working hard to get his life back on track. Maureen Kallins, Chow's attorney at the time, pointed out that Chow had developed a reputation in San Francisco's Chinatown community as a good person willing to help people in trouble. She said he was a different person when he got out of prison, a man who had improved himself through motivation and hours of Kung Fu practice.

Still, the authorities kept investigating Chow, which led to serious problems for him. For instance, he was constantly fighting Uncle Sam's efforts to deport him to Hong Kong.

Hip Sing Tong board members refused to pay the $120,000, and the next day, bullets were fired at the Hip Sing Tong headquarters. Then an ominous letter was sent to the headquarters. It was addressed to Leung and two other leaders in the Tong.

It read: "Someone open (sic) fire at your front door, but you're just chicken shit, no response to it, just keeping your mouth quiet. Having this kind of leader makes all the Tongs lose face. I have a poem to dedicate to you. It says you should be embarrassed for a thousand years and your reputation stink (sic) for ten thousand years."

Leung told authorities that Chow would not be satisfied until he killed him. Federal agents believed Leung, but they wanted him to wear a wire to further an investigation of Chow. Leung refused.

So the case died, and Leung went back to his normal life; that is, until February 2006 when a masked man entered his import-export business and demanded cash. Leung ostensibly agreed to the demand, but the robber killed him anyway with multiple shots. Leung died in front of his wife.

San Francisco's Chinese community was shocked, but nobody was willing to talk about the crime. As one prominent local Chinese leader explained, "Nobody wanted to be next."

The authorities were convinced that Raymond Chow was involved in the killing of Leung. Later, when Chow awaited charges for running the Hip Sing Tong as a criminal enterprise, William Frenzen, Assistant U.S. Attorney, would say the government had evidence Chow arranged Leung's killing. The evidence eventually presented at Chow's trial would help to expose the sordid criminal career of Raymond Chow, the infamous gangster known as "Shrimp Boy."

ꕥ

CHAPTER 1

BEGINNINGS

If anyone was born to the gangster life, it is Raymond Chow. Indeed, the more one looks at Raymond Chow's background, the more one can see that he had criminal ties that gave him much power, and he knew how to wield it.

As Chow tells it, he committed his first crime at age 8, joined the Triads and cut somebody up at age 9, and by age 12, had sex with a prostitute for the first time. In his teens, the young hoodlum was involved in a slew of criminal activities, such as gambling, extortion and racketeering.

Chow had the swagger and style of a big-time gangster, but he certainly didn't look like one, at least at first glance. Barely 5'5" tall, he had a distinctive shaved head, a pencil mustache and a penchant for white, tailor-made suits.

One of five brothers, Raymond Chow was born in Hong Kong on December 31, 1959, as Chow Kwok-Cheung. His nickname, "Shrimp Boy," an obvious reference to his short stature, was given to him by his grandmother in the belief that evil spirits could not find little children like her Raymond if they did not know their name.

Of Taishanese Chinese descent, Chow's family comes from a coastal city in the southern Guangdong province in the People's Republic of China. The number of Taishanese in China total close to a million, while another half million reside in America. The Taishanese count many notable people among their numbers, including artists, politicians, movie stars and martial artists.

Chow came to live in San Francisco, a city whose population includes 150,000 Chinese. That number amounts to about 22 percent of the population, which gives San Francisco the highest percentage of residents of Chinese descent of any major U.S. city.

Most of the Chinese live within a 20-block radius in a neighborhood known as Chinatown, the largest Chinatown outside Asia and the oldest Chinatown in the U.S. Today, San Francisco's Chinatown is a major tourist attraction, but hidden behind the glitter is a sinister side. On one hand, Chinatown is an enclave with its own customs, language, culture and institutions. On the other, it has been plagued by slums, brothels, gambling halls, and organized crime and gangs whose in-fighting has led to violence.

On the U.S. television program "Gangland," Chow said he arrived in San Francisco in 1976 and dropped out of school at age 16. Not being able to speak English, he was quickly drawn to the criminal street life. Chow later said, "As a new immigrant, I come here and I feel I don't have that security. I don't feel the safety. That's why, the first thing is, I go back to where I come. The gang."

The move to San Francisco was an easy transition for Chow. As one source put it, "He built a reputation as a brash, border-line, reckless, yet immensely respected fixture in San Francisco's Chinatown underworld. Within a year (of his arrival in San Francisco), he was entrenched at the top of the 'JU' (juvenile) criminal food chain."

Later, Chow would say, "I just want to be the best gangster, be the best fighter, no poetry, making money and also selling a lot of drugs."

How did the Shrimp Boy do as a gang member? In his unpublished memoir, Chow claimed that, after arriving in the San Francisco Bay area, he ran a brothel, organized a band of home invaders, and made $250,000 in profits from a cocaine distribution operation. In 2002, Chow boasted to a federal prosecutor, "If you are asking me which gang did I join? I did not join any gang. I owned the gang. All these people who are walking the streets of the Bay Area, all of them were controlled by me."

Chong, by all accounts, was a hard-working gangster. "After following him, he did nothing else but (work)…" revealed retired FBI special agent Joe Davidson who did surveillance on Chow for several months. "When the wire was up, that's all he did."

In his new American home, Chow did not shy away from violence. In the "Gangland" TV documentary profiling his life, Chow talked frankly about shooting a classmate from Galileo High School in the rear end. In his unpublished memoir, Chow expounded philosophically about being a gang enforcer and inflicting pain. "Beating down someone for a living is a science, ain't nothing random about it. You appraise the target for the strengths, weaknesses…inflicting injury is a delicate balance, like a recipe you season to taste. You have to be able to evaluate the level of damage you're doing while you work, and you can get pretty damn good at fighting....Most important though, you have to know when to stop."

In 1977, Chow was present at the famous Golden Dragon Restaurant Massacre on Washington Street in San Francisco, which the people of San Francisco still well remember 40 years later.

It was September 3, the Labor Day weekend, and about 100 Asian and Caucasians were dining in the popular Golden Triangle restaurant. Among the diners were ten members of the Wah Ching gang, including its leadership. The Wah Ching were allies of another gang, the Hop Sing Boys, whose Tong owned the Golden Dragon restaurant. The Wah Ching and Hop Sing Boys were locked in a bitter rivalry with a gang called the Joe Boys. Two months earlier, the Joe Boys and Wah Ching had engaged in a gun battle in which one gang member was killed and four others wounded.

Alerted that Wah Ching gang members were at the restaurant, the Joe Boys met at the home of a tattoo artist to plan a surprise attack on the enemy. They then drove to Chinatown in a stolen automobile. They wore nylon stocking masks and were heavily armed with an assortment of weapons, including a sawed off shotgun, a conventional shot gun, a .45 automatic rifle, and a .38 handgun.

The Joe Boys arrived at the scene intending to single out the Wah Ching members and kill them, but they panicked and ended up spraying the crowded restaurant with gunfire. The Wah Ching diners spotted the Joe Boys, dove behind tables for protection and began returning gunfire.

Not a single Wah Ching member was killed or injured, but five diners, including two tourists, were killed. Eleven more customers were wounded. The entire shootout took just 60 seconds.

One week later, the Wah Ching gang retaliated by killing Joe Boy Michael Lee and wounding another gang member who was shot nine times, but survived. One of the survivors of the revenge attack was Raymond Chow, not yet a notorious gangster.

The five suspects involved in the attack were caught, sentenced, and convicted for their part in the massacre. The shocking incident prompted the San Francisco Police Department to create an Asian gang unit.

Later, Chow tried to mimic the Golden Dragon Restaurant Massacre by sending gunmen to Boston to eliminate a rival gang member. The plan was to spray the restaurant with gunfire while an associate snuck up to the target's table and shot him in the head. But Chow had second thoughts and called off the hit.

The law finally caught up with Chow. At age 18, he was busted and imprisoned for robbing a group of engineers at a party. The way Chow tells the story, he was led to believe he would be sticking up a "shady parlor." When he got to the party, Chow said he pulled his gun but then realized the gathering was not what he was led to believe it would be. According to Chow, he went ahead with the robbery anyway because he had his gun drawn.

Arrested, Chow was sentenced to eleven years in prison. After serving seven years and four months, Chow was released in 1985, but he got into trouble with the law again the following year. On May 31, 1986, Chow was at a popular night club in Chinatown when a Wah Ching gang member started an altercation. After it was over, Chow was charged with 28 counts of assault with a deadly weapon, attempted murder, and illegal possession of a firearm. He received a three-year sentence.

In prison, Chow met Charles Manson, one of the most notorious mass murderers in American history. In 1971, Manson, along with several of his female compatriots, was convicted of committing seven murders. Manson was subsequently convicted of involvement in two more murders.

Ironically, no evidence exists that Manson ever killed anyone himself, but under the rules of accomplice liability, he was deemed as responsible for the killings as the actual perpetrators who caused the deaths of the nine people.

Today, Chow calls Manson a friend. "I did time with a bunch of amazing people," Chow later recalled. "Each person you talk to (you) learn something from them. Aren't no stupid people inside a prison. You can say that."

During testimony at his trial in 2015, the loquacious Chow boasted, "I'm very good with jailhouse politics. I use to run the jail. They have a riot. They come (sic) talk to me and ask my opinion. I sell drugs inside the prison. I did all that..."

Released from prison in 1989, Chow was once again back on the streets where he continued his criminal ways—smuggling drugs, running prostitution rings, and extorting money from Chinese business owners. Little did Chow know that the FBI had begun wiretapping him.

To law enforcement, Chow was a thug who, if he didn't get his way, would invariably resort to violence. In Chow's 1996 trial, U.S. Attorney William Schiffer described how Chow once ordered members of his gang to return to the scene of a crime and administer a second beating to a woman he suspected of snitching on his gang. For Chow, breaking the woman's shoulder and loosening some of her teeth during the first encounter was not enough punishment.

Chow was a charismatic gang leader, and the young gang members were eager to please him. They robbed, sold drugs, and extorted money for him without question. According to one report, "Chow's 'underlings' were caught roaming the sidewalks of Oakland's Chinatown seeking protection money from restaurant owners. One Oakland Police Department official recalled, "They were going door to door asking for money. They actually had gang members crisscrossing the street with a ledger, checking stores off as they went along."

Chow's life changed in a big way when he met Peter Chong in 1991 and became his right hand man. Known as "Uncle" in the local Chinese community, Chong controlled extortion, loan sharking, gambling, and drug trafficking. Court records show that Chong wanted to form alliances with other Chinese gangs, and he thought Chow could help him do that.

Through Chong, Chow began working with the Wo Hop To Triad, currently one of four major Triads in existence. Founded in 1908, Wo Hop To translates as "Harmonious United Association" or "Harmonious Union Plan."

Triads are the oldest and most structured of the Chinese criminal organizations and date back to the Chinese secret societies of the 17th century. According to a U.S. government investigation of Chinese criminal organizations, these societies took vows of secrecy and loyalty as a means of self- protection from the corrupt Ching dynasty.

When the Ching government collapsed in 1912 and the Republic of China was established, the Triads sometimes turned to crime while continuing to follow their self-protection rituals. The Triads are one of many branches of Chinese transnational organized crime in countries with significant Chinese populations, including the U.S. They are involved in a range of criminal activities from extortion and money laundering to prostitution and drug trafficking to health care fraud.

According to a U.S. government report, the Triad influence on the Tongs and gangs is strong, and its emphasis on order, secrecy, and loyalty creates a hurdle that is very difficult for law enforcement to penetrate.

ഇ ഗ

CHAPTER 2

MR. CHONG

Working for Peter Chong after his release from prison in 1989 was, no doubt, the major event in Raymond Chow's life. Most importantly, their relationship helped to propel Chow towards the highest echelons in the Chinese criminal underworld.

A native of Vietnam and a Chinese citizen, Peter Chong came to the U.S. in 1985, ostensibly to establish a Chinese opera company. Authorities, however, believe the Wo Hop To sent Chong to oversee their interests in the U.S. Chong was already a seasoned gangster who had previously been convicted of extortion and racketeering. In San Francisco, Chong took up where he had left off in Hong Kong.

In getting himself established in San Francisco's criminal world, Chow tried to portray himself as a legitimate businessman. However, federal investigators eventually exposed his connection to the Wo Hop To and how he took charge of its local San Francisco branch. Investigators were especially worried because it was the first time, as far as they could tell, that any Chinese Triad or criminal structure had been transferred from Asia to the U.S.

In 1991, the U.S. Senate's Permanent Subcommittee on Investigations of the Committee on Governmental Affairs conducted a six-month investigation in which they interviewed 75 law enforcement officials from around the country, as well as alleged Asian gang members and organized crime figures. The subcommittee identified Wo Hop To as being involved in heroin trafficking, illegal gambling, loan sharking, credit card fraud, among other crimes, and for being responsible for the first gangland-style killings in the San Francisco area.

In November 1991, Chong was called before the subcommittee, but he refused to testify, asserting his constitutional rights that protected him against self-incrimination. The committee's report charged that Chong controlled many gambling parlors in San Francisco's Chinatown. A Chinese businessman told the subcommittee that anybody wanting to open a gambling operation in Chinatown had to seek Chong's permission and give him a percentage of the take. The subcommittee reports revealed that Wo Hop To, under Chong's leadership, extracted up to $750 per table from more than 50 gambling parlors in San Francisco's Chinatown in return for "protection."

The subcommittee also claimed that Chong recruited about 100 underlings, between the ages of 14 to 25, and organized them into semi-military structures similar to those the Triads employed. Chong used the young kids to intimidate and terrorize local citizens, especially merchants who had refused to pay protection and the families of gamblers with bad debts.

Chong's exploitation of Chinatown's youth did not sit well with authorities. One FBI agent who investigated Chow complained to the *San Jose Mercury News:* "What you have is a very sad case of derelict criminals exploiting our young men to kill, to burn, to be drug traffickers...all for their own financial gain."

Chong always denied he was a gangster who headed the Wo Hop To. In April 1993, he appeared on CBS's "Sixty Minutes" news program and said: "I came to America, just like the other immigrants, to get my kids better education and better, free style (of) life. The law enforcement thinks that I'm involved with the Chinese organized crime because many years ago I'm running an illegal gambling house in Hong Kong."

Despite his disclaimers, Chong, no doubt, was a gangster, who ruled the Chinese underworld in the San Francisco area with an iron fist. And everybody in the city's Chinatown feared him. As a sign of that fear, anybody in Chong's gang could eat for free in any Chinatown restaurant, and no owner would complain.

Chong was good at being a gangster, and authorities were in awe of the criminal organization he had organized with Chow's assistance. The FBI compared their organization to the American mafia in terms of its sophistication.

A lot of Chong's success as a gangster could be attributed to his style. Unassuming in manner and looks, Chong was soft spoken, yet good at bringing people together. Chong knew it was smart for a gangster to keep a low profile. He avoided flashy clothing and did not flaunt his wealth. As one jewelry store owner in San Francisco's Chinatown told a local newspaper, "He had soft hands. He looked like the owner of a restaurant or retail store."

Chong worked hard to project an image of a respectable and generous businessman. He would stroll the streets, play cards in the park, and pass out business cards to merchants whenever he could. He mixed with the common man, especially those who frequented the popular gambling dens. He even helped waiters pay off their gambling debts. One former director of a Chinatown youth center said Chow was known as the "social worker gangster" because people looked at him almost like a Robin Hood who robbed the rich to give to the poor.

Not everything criminal went smoothly for Chong. He decided to establish a series of safe houses where Wo Hop To gang members could hole and stash their weapons. When police searched one of the safe houses, Chong decided the house had become a liability and it was time to cash in on its insurance policy. While he went out of town, Chong had a couple of his underlings, Andy Li and Cho Soo Li, torch the safe house.

But the arsonists botched the job, drenching the apartment with gasoline but neglecting to snuff a pilot light. They were severely burned in the process. Chow and Chong tried to deflect responsibility for the crime, telling police that their rival, the Wah Ching gang, was to blame for the fire.

Chong stayed out of the day-to-day affairs of his criminal organization. That responsibility was given to the street-tough Raymond Chow, who, unlike Chong, was in your face and extremely violent. The Shrimp Boy promised death to anyone in the organization who broke one of its loyalty oaths. He made sure the underlings were aware he knew where their family and relatives lived.

Interestingly, Chow did not think too much of the underlings. In one taped telephone conversation, Chow berated one of them for hanging out at a brothel rather than taking care of business. "Work is work," Chong chastised the underling. "You guys just can't come out for pleasure and for fight."

Yet, underlings in the Chong-Chow organization seemed to respect Chow. After all, he had walked the walk and appeared to be an authentic gangster. One former member of the Chong-Chow organization recalled how Chow would tell the underlings in his organization, "You guys are all brothers. You should not be afraid to go to prison. It's kind of good to be going to prison. You may even die."

As Wo Hop To grew in power under the leadership of the Chong-Chow alliance, it became apparent to other gangs in the San Francisco area that they would have to either join or face the consequences. Certain criminal elements in Chinatown, however, resisted. One of them was Danny Wong, the head of the Wah Ching gang. There was bad blood between Chong and Wong, and their dispute became personal and violent

After finding his closest bodyguard dead, Wong desperately fought back against the Wo Hop To and tried to kill a car load of their members by unleashing a barrage of gun fire outside a club in San Francisco's North Beach district. A few moments later, another person fired on a second group of Wo Hop To members, killing two and injuring eight.

The tension grew, but Wong knew he could not win the war. So he offered to meet with Chong to work out a truce. Chong agreed, and they met at a restaurant where Chong actually made a toast at a banquet being held there. It looked as if the bitter dispute had been smoothed out, but in less than a year, Wong was dead from a bullet in his head. Chong, with Chow as his right-hand man, was now in control of San Francisco's criminal underworld.

Chow and Chong began to look beyond San Francisco and planned on organizing a national syndicate, or what they called Tien Ha Wu (the Whole Earth Society). The name Tien Ha Wu, or Whole Earth Society, comes from a comic book story of super villains joining forces to conquer the world. The syndicate would include all the Asian gangs in the U.S., with Chow as the leader. Chong and Chow planned to make a lot of money, while at the same time expanding their powerbase.

Chong sent an emissary to Boston to establish a foothold, but Chinese organized crime was controlled by Wayne Kwong and his former partner Bike Ming, two well-entrenched Chinese gangsters. Wayne Kwong agreed to join forces with Chong and Chow, but Bike Ming refused.

In 1991 Chong and Chow met with Kwong to see if they could work together to promote their mutual interests. Later at trial, Chow explained through a translator, "We tried to extend our authority from West Coast. We all understood that he (Chong) would be the leader, and we would be in charge of East Coast operations. It was brought up by Chong, then Wayne and I agreed to it."

Chong, Chow, and Kwong agreed that Ming was an obstacle to their plans, and they formed an alliance to get rid of him. Chong and Chow sent two teenage hit men to Kwong with instructions on how to kill Ming. But when the teenagers saw a policeman in a restaurant where the hit was to take place, they froze and decided not to go through with it.

Meanwhile Chong, Chow, and Kwong went ahead with a plan that involved the large-scale distribution of drugs across the U.S. According to the plan, the alliance would import heroin from Taiwan through Philadelphia, then take drug shipments to Atlantic City before moving them to the San Francisco area.

The plan, however, never took off. By now, the authorities were moving in to bust the Chong-Chow organization. Raymond Chow tried to make a $100,000 cocaine buy for the group, but made the mistake of trying to arrange the deal with an undercover DEA agent. All of Chow's and Chong's big plans to conquer the drug trade in the name of the Whole Earth Society were about to fall apart.

ﾂｫ ﾂｻ

CHAPTER 3

SETBACK

Raymond Chow and Peter Chong thought they were infallible, but they did not count on law enforcement's persistent efforts to take them down. In 1992, Chong fled to Hong Kong before being indicted on the charge of helping to mastermind Boston gangster Bike Ming's murder. The indictment was the culmination of a three-year investigation of Chow and Chong and their criminal organization. It was the first racketeering indictment on the West Coast against Asian organized crime.

The Hong Kong authorities arrested Chong after he arrived, but released him when they concluded that Uncle Sam had not provided convincing evidence for his extradition. Chong continued to fight extradition, maintaining that he would not get a fair trial in the U.S.A. because of his race.

Raymond Chow was already in custody. FBI agents arrested him and five other associates in Boston, New York City, and Atlantic City, New Jersey, on drug charges. All six men were arrested just as a drug deal was about to go down at a casino in Atlantic City. The arrests stemmed from a year-long investigation into Chinese organized crime by the FBI, the San Francisco Police Department, and the California Department of Justice. The feds believed they had enough evidence on Chow to indict him on racketeering charges. The authorities had used numerous wiretaps to intercept conversations between the suspects.

Interestingly, the charges against Chow were separated into two trials, one for illegal gun sales and the other for prostitution, drugs, and money laundering. The weapons involved were Intratec "Tec-9s," 9mm semiautomatics designed to resemble small machine gun pistols. Two of the weapons were seized during an attempted computer store robbery in Milpitas, California. Other guns were taken from members of the "Underlings," a criminal organization that Chow allegedly organized as a Hop Sing Tong youth group.

In the first trial, Chow was indicted along with nineteen others in a forty-eight count superseding indictment and charged with heroin and cocaine trafficking, loan sharking, extortion, prostitution, gun running, and murder for hire. Upon motion of the defendants, seven counts dealing with firearms violations were severed from the remaining counts and renumbered one through seven. These counts named Chow, along with co-defendants Au Shek Kan, Sophie Han, Lei Guo Tai, and Wayne Kwong. Han and Kwong plead guilty prior to trial. Kan and Tai changed their pleas to guilty after the trial started.

The prosecution of 25-year-old Andy Li, a Chow co-defendant, was separated from the case. Li was separated because he was under heavy medication for pain, the result of the plastic surgery he had to undergo to repair the burn scars suffered in the September 1991 arson fire. He was to be tried at a later date on racketeering charges.

In Chow's first trial, the evidence offered by the government consisted of thirty transcripts of telephone conversations, the testimony of cooperating co-defendants, and the numerous weapons seized from co-defendant Kan and others. The evidence showed that Chow was a leader of the Hop Sing Tong gang, which consisted of approximately one hundred members. He had provided firearms to members of the gang, procuring them primarily from Kan, the leader of the gang's Portland, Oregon, chapter.

When the case came to trial on February 28, 1995, the prosecutor and Chow's attorney presented two highly contrasting views of the defendant. To the prosecution, Chow was a powerful and ambitious criminal master mind whose goal was to take over organized crime in Chinese communities across the U.S. The defense, on the other hand, portrayed Chow as a misunderstood victim, a Kung-Fu master who was known in Chinatown for helping others. The defense even tried to use the race card, insinuating that Chow was being prosecuted because of the color of his skin.

"He is not part of the criminal element," said Maureen Kallins, Chow's defense attorney. "He's not part of any of this. The transcripts of the wiretaps will exonerate him."

In testifying in court, Chow claimed, "I never introduce (sic) anyone to doing crime. People offer me drug, different business opportunity (sic)… they call me, they offer me back in the business. They want me back in the business. I tell them no. I put a lot of people together, and they get to know each other, for the good time party."

In February 1995, after a jury trial lasting two weeks, Chow was found guilty and convicted on all counts of conspiracy and of dealing in firearms without a license, shipping weapons across a state border, interstate shipment of firearms by a convicted felon, and importation of firearms with knowledge they would be used in the commission of crimes.

Chow was cleared of the count 5 charge of transporting firearms with obliterated serial numbers. He was sentenced to a term of incarceration of 280 months to be followed by three years supervised release, a fine of $47,500 and a $300 special assessment.

"With the conviction of Raymond Chow this day, this office has now convicted the heads of major Asian organized crime groups in three major American cities," said U.S. Attorney Michael Yamaguchi, whose San Francisco office supervised the case.

Chow and more than a dozen other defendants still awaited trial on the racketeering charges filed in October 1993. A 140-page indictment in that case charged Chow and others with conspiracy, heroin trafficking, contract murder, extortion and arson for profit.

The government was not as fortunate when they tried the second case against Chow. His trial took a month to complete during which time the prosecution presented transcripts from scores of telephone wiretaps and testimony from associates and employees of Chow's alleged crime organization. Kallins, Chow's attorney, claimed during the trial that federal prosecutors were conducting a federal vendetta against her client and that the only evidence had come from gangsters who had agreed to testify so they could get off with lesser sentences for their crimes.

"Our position was that the government cheated in an effort to get Mr. Chow," Kallins charged. "They (prosecutors) invented evidence. They used convicted criminals as witnesses against him (Chow)."

In May 1996, the federal government suffered a major blow when the racketeering trial against Raymond Chow was declared a mistrial. The jury had deliberated for six hours before two jurors sent a note to the judge stating that a verdict was impossible. The two jurors believed Chow should have been cleared of all charges. It had taken weeks of deliberation for the jury to reach a nearly even split decision.

Defense Attorney Kallins was quick to claim victory. "Federal authorities spent $10 million to get this guy, and they couldn't get him on any of the 48 counts," she told the media.

U.S. Attorney Michael Yamaguchi said that the government definitely intended to appeal the case. He found it strange that all the other suspects named in the original indictment of Chow had been convicted of the charges by other juries or had entered guilty pleas. The prosecution tried to sound upbeat, noting that Chow had already been convicted of six counts of trafficking arms.

On January 8, 2016, Chow was found guilty on all 162 counts, including one count of murder, which carries a life sentence. Raymond Chow, no doubt, was going to prison, but when the sentence finally came, it still was devastating. On 4, 2016, Chow was sentenced to two life terms. Raymond's life as a big time gangster was over.

ꕤ ꕤ

PHOTOS

Raymond Chow

San Francisco China Town

Raymond Chow relaxing

Funeral of Allen Leung
Prominent Chinatown businessman gunned down in 2006 with his wife present

Peter Chong – AKA "Uncle"
Controlled extortion, loan sharking, gambling, and drug trafficking

Tony Serra
Lead Lawyer in Mr. Chow's defense team

ꟾ ☙ ❧

CHAPTER 4

INFORMANT

Chow was now in prison for what looked like a long time. Meanwhile, Chong managed to elude U.S. authorities for eight years. Then in May 2000, the Hong Kong government made a remarkable gesture of good will. It extradited Chong to the U.S.

Chow did not particularly like the fact that his partner Chong had fled to Hong Kong and left him to face the music. It was not that he resented Chong's self-preservation move. He could understand that. It was just that he did not like Chong's effort, as Chow saw it, to have his underlings put "everything on him." Whether that was true or not, Chow faced many more years in prison, and he had a lot of time to think about how he got there.

As Chow stewed, the authorities worked hard to convince him to rat out his former partner. They viewed Chong's upcoming trial as one of the most important in the history of Asian organized crime in the U.S. As one Oakland, California, police inspector told the *San Jose Mercury News,* "Convicting Chong would be a milestone in Asian organized crime investigations."

Eventually, the authorities succeeded in flipping Chow, and he became the federal government's star witness in Chong's trial. The deal—Chow's testimony for a reduced sentence.

But Chong did not plan on going down without a fight. He proclaimed his innocence to the press. He had never killed anybody, Chong claimed. Nor had he peddled drug or extorted money. Chow was a liar, a criminal who cut a deal with Uncle Sam to save his own skin, Chong complained to the press.

The six-week trial began in March, 2015. When Chow took the stand, Chong's defense team focused on what they claimed was the "sweetheart deal" Chow had cut with Uncle Sam to ensure that the jury would understand it. Chow was sentenced in 1996 to 24 years in federal prison, but the "sweetheart deal" would have the gangster released in June 2015, where upon he would be given a new identity.

Chow's testimony made for good theatre. Under cross examination, Chow spoke through a Cantonese translator. He was on the stand for hours as the defense tried to break him down, but the egocentric Chow held his own. Nor did he shy away from blabbing about his prominent role in Chong's organization. He portrayed himself as Chong's partner involved in their organization's decision making.

Chow confirmed that Chong was head of the Wo Hop To and involved in a wide range of crimes, including extortion, gambling, and drug trafficking. Chow testified about how he and Chong had allied themselves with Boston gangster Wayne Kwong and prepared to organize a nationwide umbrella group for Chinese organized crime called the Tien Ha Wu, or Whole Earth Association. "We understood that Chong would be the leader, the head," Chow testified.

Chow proved to be a persuasive witness. It took the jury three-and-a-half- days of deliberation to convict Chong of most of the charges against him. He was sentenced to 11 and 1/2 years in jail. Defense Attorney Alan Caplan described the verdict as being "totally without foundation. It's beyond anything either Bill Ostenhoudt (co-counsel) or I have experienced in 30 years of practice."

Caplan complained that the jury must have been influenced by racial bias and said he planned to appeal the case. Predictably, the prosecution agreed with the decision. "We believe the jury acted professionally and carefully reached a just result," said U.S. Attorney David W. Shapiro.

so cs

CHAPTER 5

COMEBACK

With his release in 2003 Raymond Chow was back on the street. Uncle Sam did not return his visa, nor did they give him witness protection as part of his plea arrangement. Chow claimed that the government had promised him witness protection, but it had never followed up. Chow sounded a little paranoid when he surmised that the feds may have wanted him on the street as "bait" to lure gangsters who wanted to seek revenge.

Chow had to wear an ankle monitor, which he did for nearly 10 years. He was also required to dutifully check in with immigration officials three times a week. Perhaps toughest of all the regulations Chow had to follow was the one forbidding him from making any kind of cash.

Chow had to watch his step, but he admitted that his gangster reputation made for a tough transition from the gangster life. "When I come out of jail and I walk (down the street), everybody is scared to say hi to me," he said. "Nobody really wants to talk."

Chow's supporters noted that he had done an outstanding job in court testifying against Chong and had earned the deal he made with law enforcement. But some law enforcement officials familiar with Chow's criminal career warned that society was taking a big risk by allowing Chow back on the street. "He's the worst of the worst," Ignatius Chinn, a California Department of Justice special agent, told a television station. "They made a deal with the devil and now the devil's out."

Many in law enforcement still believed that Chow had something to do with the murder of Allen Leung, the prominent Chinatown businessman gunned down in 2006 with his wife present. Chow repeatedly denied any knowledge of the killing and claimed he had no control over gang members who wanted to use his name in an extortion attempt. Despite the suspicions, Chow had the nerve to show up at Leung's funeral. Remarkably, he was allowed to bow in front of Leung's casket, a sign of honor in the Chinese community.

Meanwhile, Chow continued to work hard to change the public's perception of him. First of all, he changed his appearance. He still wore a couple of earrings in one ear, but he opted for conservative dress and a clean-shaven image in which his prominent tattoos were barely visible.

Whenever he had the opportunity, he publicly vowed to lead a criminal-free life. To show that his intentions were good, Chow spent a lot of his time informing young people in San Francisco about the importance of education. Chow pointed to himself as an example of missed opportunity, revealing that he only had a third grade education and could barely speak or write in English. He did his best to motivate youngsters to stay away from gangs, drugs, and violence. He shared his life encounters and experiences with young people to persuade them to remain on life's straight and narrow path.

Chow became active in civic affairs. For instance, he became the head of Hung Moon Ghee Kong Tong, a fraternal organization in San Francisco occasionally referred to as the Chinese Freemasons.

Chow even reached out to businesses and advised them on how they could prevent crime.

Later in court, Chow admitted that he was not totally "clean" during the time he spent on the street after his 2003 release. "Let me clean up something," Chow testified. "I get a party. Sometime I snort a couple of bump. I don't know if you consider that legal, but for me, it's very normal just for a party. It's normal to me."

Numerous documentaries featuring the "new" Raymond "Shrimp Boy" Chow aired. They included Gangland's "Deadly Triangle" on the History channel, "Chinatown Mafia" on National Geographic, and a special on Channel Five: 30 Mins Bay Area, "The Man in White." Chow's story even appeared on Gangland's "Most Notorious OG," as narrated by gangster rap artists Snoop Dogg and Ice-T.

He also completed a special interview with Alan Wang titled "Bay Area Gangster Turns Celebrity," which aired on San Francisco television. The "reformed" gangster even found time to complete his unpublished memoir and speak with several Hollywood producers and publishers about it and the possibility of motion picture projects.

Chow's campaign at rehabilitation appeared to be working. He became popular with a segment of the San Francisco's public. As one reporter described his experience with Chow, "Each time we walked together around Chinatown, Chow was met with smiles and greetings called out from street corners and shop windows. Many called him "Big Brother" or "Dai Lo!" The greeting, "Dai Lo," could be taken to mean "love" or "respect," but in the world of Asian organized crime it could also mean "crime boss."

Not everybody was impressed with the "reformed" Chow. Shrimp Boy was not paranoid. A lot of individuals who came in contact with him did indeed feel uneasy. Aaron Poskin, a former San Francisco city supervisor, recalled for the San Jose Mercury News newspaper sitting next to Chow at a banquet: "Despite his affable laugh and high-pitched voice, I got a very bad vibe off the guy. He can be intimidating. When I walked away from him, I remember thinking, “This is a dangerous, seething human being. Diabolical is exactly the word.”

Others did not like Chow walking around San Francisco as if he was a celebrity. They disliked the proclamations that politicians were willing to give to Chow like an adult gave candy to a baby. In 2012, for instance, Diane Feinstein, the U.S. Senator from California, issued a statement recognizing Chow as a former offender who had become a big asset in the community.

Many locales wondered how he could afford the expensive cars he drove and clothes he wore. After all, he was supposed to be broke. Chow claimed a family friend had sold the motorcycle to him at a nice discount. Still, Chow’s explanation was hard to reconcile with the image of him on his Facebook page wearing an expensive suit and sitting on the expensive black motorcycle.

So, yes, Chow had supporters, but he also had a lot of detractors who wondered if Chow would stay out of prison.

ഌ ഁ

CHAPTER 6

ARREST

On March 26, 2014, came a shocker of an announcement: the arrest of California State Senator Leland Yee on bribery and corruption charges. Raymond Chow was back in the news in a big way. The U.S. government released a 137-page indictment that charged Raymond Chow and 24 others with money laundering and other crimes. The Federal Bureau of Investigation (FBI) had arrested Chow during a raid that was part of a larger investigation connected to Asian-American crime.

Leland Yee was a pillar of the San Francisco community. Born on November 20, 1948, Yee had immigrated to San Francisco, California, from his birthplace of Taishan, Guangdong, China, when he was three years old. He later became a naturalized American citizen. After obtaining his doctorate in child psychology, Yee worked as a therapist in the Mental Health Department of the City of San Francisco, the Oakland School District, and Asian American for Community Involvement, a non-profit that serves low-income people.

There was a hint of trouble when Yee was arrested in 1992 for allegedly shoplifting a bottle of tanning oil from a supermarket. But the case was not prosecuted. Yee disappeared before he could be arrested. Then in 1999, Yee was stopped twice by police for suspicion of soliciting prostitutes in San Francisco's Mission District. But nothing happened.

Those incidents, though, did not stop Yee from rising politically. He became a California State Assemblyman, a supervisor with the San Francisco's Sunset District and the President of the San Francisco School Board. In 2004 Yee became the first Asian American to be appointed Speaker Pro Tempore, making him the second highest ranking Democrat in the California State Assembly. In 2006, he became a state senator. At the time of his arrest, Yee was a candidate for the office of Secretary for State, but he withdrew from the race after his arrest.

Yee was known as a prominent gun control advocate. In February 2013, Yee claimed to have received a death threat from a trained marine sniper who objected to Yee's actions in support of gun control. Everett Basham, 45, was arrested in February 2013, and later pleaded no contest to the charges.

Yee's arrest was particularly shocking because the criminal complaint charged that Yee and an intermediary had met repeatedly with an undercover agent to solicit campaign contributions in exchange for setting up a deal with intermediary arms dealers. "It seems like nobody knew this was coming, and everyone is astounded by the allegations," Corey Cook, director of the University of San Francisco's Leo T. McCarthy Center for Public Service and the Common Good, told the Pleasanton, California-based *Valley Herald* newspaper. "Political corruption is one thing, but this is a whole other level."

The criminal complaint revealed that Chow had been in the sights of Uncle Sam ever since his release from prison in 2003. Undercover agents had infiltrated Chow's criminal enterprise and the Ghee Kung Tong fraternal organization, of which Chow was the leader known as "Dragon Head."

The criminal complaint identified an undercover agent involved in the investigation as UCE 4599. Later, the alias "David Jordan" was used to identify him. Jordan introduced himself to Chow as a member of La Cosa Nostra who had come out West to manage the mob's illegal gambling organization.

Jordan, a former military man, spent three years working undercover. He even broke the law to get close to Chow and his organization in the hope he could catch them in the criminal act. Over time, the agent gained Chow's trust to the point where he became a "consultant" to Chow's Tong. The complaint noted that, while Chow claimed he went clean after his prison release in 2003, he admitted during Jordan's undercover work of approving all criminal activity in the Tong.

As the Chow-Jordan relationship developed, Chow tried to have it both ways. He refused to get involved directly with gun trafficking, drug running, or money laundering, but he was willing to make introductions to facilitate deals in exchange for cash from the undercover FBI agent. In one wiretapped conversation, Chow revealed his strategy: by being the target of law enforcement, other members of the organization could conduct criminal activity "freely."

Chow introduced Jordan to Keith Jackson, a former school board president and San Francisco political consultant, telling the FBI agent that Jackson could do "inside deals" with the city. Jackson became the go-between from Chow to Leland Yee.

Jackson tried to get Jordan to donate money to Yee's mayoral campaign, but Jordan put Jackson in touch with another undercover agent who gave money to Jackson's consulting firm, which was ostensibly meant for Yee's mayoral campaign.

Yee received money for favors. In one instance, Yee arranged meetings with two senators for $21,000.

The criminal complaint included the charge that money was exchanged for arranging international arms deals. According to the complaint, Jackson arranged a meeting with one international arms trafficker who "was attempting to ship weapons to the Philippines where there was an on-going war between an unidentified Muslim group and the Philippines government." Jackson boasted that he had known the international arms dealer for years and that just one arms deal could be worth $2.5 million. Yee told Jordan he could supply automatic weapons but wasn't sure if he could do the same for shoulder-fired missiles.

In meetings with the undercover agent, Yee revealed he knew much about the international arms trade. He described Africa as "a largely untapped market for trade" and said he could travel to the Philippines to help arrange a deal.

The conspiracy was not limited to arms trafficking. Jackson, his son, Brandon, and an associate conspired in the sale of fraudulent credit cards, cocaine, and even planned a murder-for-hire scheme.

Everything was for sale, as far as Yee was concerned. For instance, he sold a proclamation honoring Chow's Ghee Kung Tong for $6,800.

While Yee, Chow, and Jackson were the prime catches in the undercover sting, there were some other interesting defendants. Marlon Darrell Sullivan was an Oakland-based sports agent who, for a short time, was an advisor to Michael Sam, the University of Missouri football player who announced he was gay. The NFL Players Association suspended Sullivan for being linked to making of illicit payments to a former college football player.

Another defendant, Wilson Lim, was a 60-year-old dentist who, according to the complaint, was involved in illegally importing firearms. George Nieh, 44, was Chow's driver and one of his most trusted associates. In the complaint, he was identified as the primary contact between Chow and Yee.

Chow's legal team was led by noted lawyer Tony Serra, who, in a Vice.com profile, was described as the "Hippy Atticus Finch," a reference to the fictional lawyer who represented the black man in Harper Lee's classic novel, *To Kill a Mocking Bird*.

Serra is considered to be one of America's best lawyers and certainly one of its most colorful and outspoken. Serra once boasted, "I'm one of the last of a dying breed. Most defense lawyers are negotiators nowadays. I'm not!"

In his take-no-prisoners style, Serra charged that Chow was being selectively prosecuted. San Francisco Mayor Ed Lee had been implicated in wrong-doing by undercover stings. Yet, nothing had happened. At the time, Lee was running for re-election, and through his campaign spokesman, Lee denied he had done anything inappropriate.

On July 1, 2015, Yee, Keith Jackson, Brandon Jackson, and Marlon Sullivan pled guilty to racketeering and bribery charges. By pleading guilty, the 68-year old Yee avoided going to trial in August 2015. He admitted to taking payments in return for promises that he would use his political position in the service of a variety of powerful interests. In February 2016, Yee was sentenced to five years in prison.

As Chow's trial began, the respective strategies of the prosecution and defense became apparent. The prosecution argued that Chow's so called "good works" in the community were nothing more than a ruse for Chow and his associates to pursue criminal schemes, including drug trafficking, plotting murders, and laundering money.

Chow's lawyers, on the other hand, argued that the FBI had entrapped Chow and badgered him until he took dirty money. They further contended that the judge was biased against their client from the start. The defense intimated cover up, pointing out that the judge refused to consider evidence implicating city officials.

The prosecution introduced hours of audio and video recordings gleaned from the undercover operation. To trial observers, many of the recordings clearly showed Chow talking about criminal activity and accepting money for arranging deals. The lead FBI undercover agent, who testified under the pseudonym David Jordan to protect his identity, testified that Chow repeatedly took money from money launderers to whom he had introduced him.

In an unusual move, Chow took the stand on December 21, 2015, to convince the jury that he had been on the straight and narrow road since his release from prison in 2003. In a statement, Curtis Briggs, a Chow lawyer, explained Chow's appearance on the witness stand. "Chow is confident after weeks of fabricated testimony by government conspirators. He wants his story told and does not feel the need to wait any longer."

Chow acknowledged to the court room that his pre-2003 life was soaked in cocaine, but he claimed that the racketeering indictment against him was a "fiction."

To rebut Chow's testimony, the prosecution quoted passages from Chow's unpublished memoir, which seemingly contradicted Chow's claims of innocence that he did not know about what his associates were doing. Chow said he stood by his statements in the book, but steadfastly denied knowledge of any wrong doing. At one point, Assistant U.S. Attorney William Frentzen chided Chow: "Are you a Dragon Head or are you a sucker?"

The trial finally ended after months of testimony. On January 8, 2016, Chow, dressed in black sports coat and tie, stood in court to hear the verdict. He stared straight ahead and showed no emotion as the verdict announced guilt on all 162 counts of murder, racketeering, and other crimes.

Vowing to appeal, Chow's defense team sounded optimistic, citing irregularities in the trial as they saw them. Sentencing was scheduled for March 23, 2016, but it was postponed, and Judge Charles Breyer set April 15 as the deadline for Chow's lawyers to submit post-trial motions. Judge Breyer said he would set the sentencing date later.

Whenever that happened, there seemed little doubt that Chow would lose his appeal and spend the rest of his days in prison.

Raymond's Chow conviction, no doubt, would have a long-term impact. His trial had opened up a veritable Pandora's Box. Both the investigation and the trial showed that San Francisco was a corrupt metropolis. More investigations had been opened while the Raymond Chow saga played out, and still more were expected to be opened.

The big question: Would any of them connect to Raymond Chow? Whatever the answer, it was all but certain that the saga of the Shrimp Boy was not over.

ഇ ര ഇ ര

Index

ꟸ ꟸ ꟸ